HOW TO START A
REVOLUTION

YOUNG PEOPLE AND THE
FUTURE OF AMERICAN POLITICS

LAUREN DUCA

SIMON & SCHUSTER PAPERBACKS

NEW YORK LONDON TORONTO SYDNEY NEW DELHI

Simon & Schuster Paperbacks
An Imprint of Simon & Schuster, Inc.
1230 Avenue of the Americas
New York, NY 10020

Copyright © 2019 by Lauren Duca

All rights reserved, including the right to reproduce this book or portions thereof in
any form whatsoever. For information, address Simon & Schuster Subsidiary Rights
Department, 1230 Avenue of the Americas, New York, NY 10020.

First Simon & Schuster trade paperback edition September 2020

SIMON & SCHUSTER PAPERBACKS and colophon are registered
trademarks of Simon & Schuster, Inc.

For information about special discounts for bulk purchases, please contact Simon &
Schuster Special Sales at 1-866-506-1949 or business@simonandschuster.com.

The Simon & Schuster Speakers Bureau can bring authors to your live event. For
more information or to book an event, contact the Simon & Schuster Speakers Bureau
at 1-866-248-3049 or visit our website at www.simonspeakers.com.

Interior design by Carly Loman

Manufactured in the United States of America

10   9   8   7   6   5   4   3   2   1

Library of Congress Cataloging-in-Publication Data is available.

ISBN 978-1-5011-8163-4
ISBN 978-1-5011-8164-1 (pbk)
ISBN 978-1-5011-8165-8 (ebook)

For Laura

CONTENTS

HOW TO START A
REVOLUTION

THE BEFORE TIMES

Before the 2016 election, I only ever understood politics as a spectator sport. Actually, watching football is a frighteningly accurate metaphor for the way I learned about politics growing up. Every four years, everyone would gather around for the election, or as I came to understand it, "the big game." There were teams, and little reason to deviate from whichever one to which you had previously pledged loyalty. Without intricate knowledge of the inner workings of the sport, you might watch along with passive interest, mostly to see who was going to win. (Also, obviously, the men were always yelling louder than anyone else.)

I suppose I first understood my parents were Republicans when my mom told me that I should vote for Bob Dole in a mock version of the 1996 election at my elementary school. I can still smell the marinade of low-grade sloppy joe meat in the cafeteria on that day. I remember standing in front of a big box covered in aluminum foil, staring at the paper ballot featuring Bill Clinton (Democrat) and Bob Dole (Republican), along with a portrait of each. Waiting on the line leading up to the table,

I decided that, actually, I liked the other guy better. (I'd love to tell you I was developing a fiery political ideology in kindergarten, but that came later. Mostly Bob looked super old.)

Not long after that mock version of the 1996 election, I knew that I was cheering for the other team. During my junior year of high school, I learned that seven in ten children go on to affiliate with the same party as their parents. I definitely thought, "Not me, Gallup Poll."

My worldview has long been rooted in a desire to leave the world a better place than I found it. Before I had access to the word "feminism" or was introduced to the wide-reaching effects of institutionalized racism, I understood true equality to be the highest possible good. This was precisely as complex as my unquestioned support for LGBTQ rights, which developed well before I began to understand my own sexuality as a queer woman. My views have become more nuanced over time, but I have always believed in the necessity of equity with total conviction, and that ethical priority was as simple as the fact that I had so many gay friends in high school my parents called me Liza Minnelli. (Media illiteracy has warped the concept of "bias," but if you would like to say I am biased toward equality, I'm okay with that. I'd go one step further and argue that establishing equity ought to be the ultimate mission of any true democracy, but we'll get to that later.)

My parents were confounded by my passion for social justice, evidenced, in part, by the massive pride flag hanging in my bedroom during the fight to legalize gay marriage. They were confused by my literal and figurative flag waving. We never talked about that, because as far as my mom and dad were concerned, political issues were something that could be swept out of view. In the rare instances when they dedicated energy to politics, they prioritized economic policy, which is to say, they showed up every four years to vote Republican because of the tax breaks.

I disagreed with their ideology, but I usually accepted their attitude. I avoided talking about politics growing up, too. My parents, brother, and I are textbook hotheads when we're around one another. (People often explain this to me by saying it's because we're Italian, as if our blood has been replaced with very spicy red sauce.) When my mom and dad told me to stop talking about politics, they were mostly hoping we would have one less thing to yell about.

Still, the stigmatization of political discussion was not specific to my household. In various settings of suburban New Jersey, the adults in the room were wary of the tensions that might arise. Engaging in political conversation was as crass as showing up for the neighborhood Super Bowl party without a chilled bottle of pinot grigio. This became more obvious as I grew older, but it started early. When we role-played the 1996 election, my kindergarten teacher reprimanded me for asking who she was going to vote for. Such was the sentiment echoed through my upbringing. All of the authority figures in my life believed that talking about politics was off-limits. It was meant to be private. What if—gasp—you found that you didn't agree about Bob Dole? From early on, I broke with my mom and dad over ideology, but for a long time I subscribed to the idea that avoiding political conversation altogether was simply a matter of politeness.

I was too young to vote for Obama in 2008, but that didn't stop me from trekking to Washington, DC, for his inauguration in January 2009. My friend Allen and I were so cold, we lined our gloves and socks with heating packets. Obama was barely visible in the distance, but we were too excited to care. The crowd around us was high on hope. I thought the entirety of the National Mall might lift up into the heavens as Aretha Franklin sang "My Country, 'Tis of Thee." I was thrilled to see the march toward progress going so well, and yet still didn't comprehend that it wouldn't continue unless each and every citizen chose to play an active role in our democracy. That role requires us to talk about politics.

Politics was once framed as if it might be removed from the stuff of our daily lives, as if it were, at most, a special interest. Once upon a time it was possible to say "I don't like politics," as if expressing a distaste for olives. But the 2016 election revealed that every element of our daily lives is political. The constant scandal associated with Trump's campaign and administration made political news a centerpiece of American life. We were increasingly exposed to the inner workings of the federal government. And as a result, there was elevated public awareness around the mechanics of power that dictate life in this country. We saw how politics affects where and how you vote, the quality of your local school system, and that jammed-up intersection that always makes you late for work; it determines everything—even the quality of the water we drink and the air we breathe (shout-out to that greedy little Earth pillager Scott Pruitt). Now saying "I don't like politics" is as absurd as declaring "I'm just not that into the weather."

This, as you can imagine, made things even more difficult at home. The shift began during the 2016 primaries, as it became increasingly difficult to avoid strong opinions. By the time the debates rolled around, maybe the only person in the country without a stance on Trump's candidacy was Ken Bone. But I couldn't know for sure how my parents felt about the election, because they banned political conversation by the middle of primary season.

I visited my parents' house in New Jersey during the Democratic National Convention when Hillary Clinton received the nomination. Before I arrived, my mom asked me to please "keep it nice"—she didn't want to hear all that political stuff. I excused myself after a quietly tense dinner to watch the live stream on my laptop. Hidden under the blankets in my childhood bedroom, I cried into my dusty floral duvet cover. I was moved by the possibility of a female president and disturbed by the fact that my parents were rooting against that outcome. I wished I could talk to them about it.

Throughout the campaign, I swept these feelings away. I told myself that it didn't really matter: Jersey goes blue every election. The Electoral College would render my parents' votes null and void, even if Clinton's presidency weren't all but guaranteed.

In fact, I was so sure Clinton would win, I wrote an article anticipating her victory. In October of 2016, then–*Teen Vogue* editor Amanda Chan reached out to see if I'd be down to prepare a post titled "We Just Elected Our First Female President. Here's Why That Matters."

"This is under the assumption, of course, that Hillary wins,"

5

she added. "If she does not, we'll obviously still pay you for the piece even if we're unable to run!"

"Oh GOD, don't jinx us!" I wrote back.

"HA! Knocking on all the wood, right now," Amanda responded. "Thanks, Lauren!"

A few days later, I sent Amanda a draft. I concluded the piece by declaring victory for women: "This is a hallmark occasion in the fight for women's rights no matter what happens in the next four, eight, or sixteen years. It's a giant leap toward the excruciatingly gradual process of normalization. The true victory will be far quieter. It will require no balloons or happy tears. It will feel like a natural extension of the fact that women are half of the population—no more exciting or revolutionary than electing a William, George, or John." I had no idea that I was going to have to accept that kill fee.

On November 8, 2016, I voted for Hillary Clinton in New Jersey, where I was still registered. On the train ride to my parents' house that morning, I cranked up my headphones and noted the blue water sparkling brighter than ever before. I stared out the window making a theatrically determined expression, because Hillary was going to be our next president, and also because I was pretending to be in a music video. I wasn't worried about the results. The only thing making me nervous was the possibility that my parents were going to vote for Trump.

I hoped their plan was to sit this one out—but of course, talking about politics was still off-limits. They weren't vocal Trump supporters, but I noticed they had begun to see him as "the lesser of two evils"—a refrain requiring Simone Biles–caliber mental gymnastics. I had known, since kindergarten, that my parents tended to vote for whoever was wearing the right jersey, but Trump was so monstrous, I thought this time might be an exception.

My heart sank as I pulled up to my parents' house. My dad's car was in the driveway. That meant he had come home early from work to vote.

"Hey, cookie," my dad said as I walked into the kitchen. He held out his arms for a hug. I put down my bag and begrudgingly leaned into his chest.

"Do you want something to eat?" my mom asked, opening the refrigerator to take inventory. "I made that iced coffee you like."

I stared at them like they were strangers. Throughout the campaign, I had foolishly reduced Trump supporters to backwoods Nazis, and then here were two of them, standing across from me in the kitchen, offering hugs and snacks.

I put down my bag and I placed two hands on the kitchen counter to brace myself. I was about to break the rules and talk about politics. "Please, don't do this," I said. "Don't vote for him."

My parents come from working-class backgrounds. They grew up in Queens. My mom was the only child of a divorced single mother, at a time when divorce was so taboo there were kids who weren't allowed to play with her. She put herself through community college, eventually becoming a physical therapist. My dad's parents were aggressively blue-collar. My grandpa actually lost part of an appendage working in the Scholastic factory. He's missing about a quarter of his index finger—it's some serious Upton Sinclair shit. From those humble beginnings, my dad hustled to become the vice president of a waste management company, and now he makes so much money, his political views are centered around tax breaks for the wealthy.

My mom and dad know the value of hard work, and that is perhaps the fundamental flaw in their conservatism. They believe everyone can and should struggle to obtain the American dream. What they fail to fully comprehend is that we do not all start on an even playing field. The myth of meritocracy valorizes skill and perseverance while ignoring the ways identity and class factor into success. But I wasn't supposed to talk about that with them, either.

That day, more than any other day, I imagine my dad was ready for a fight. "You are not going to tell me who to vote for," he bellowed. "Who the hell do you think you are?"

"Ralph, there is no need to yell," my mother said, wringing her hands.

"I'm not yelling!" he yelled.

"You're yelling," I said.

Then my mom turned to me. "Please don't start a fight about this stuff again," she said.

"I can't stand here and watch you vote for Donald Trump," I told her. "Haven't you seen how racist and sexist he is? Doesn't that mean anything to you?"

My dad began to grumble.

"I told you that you were welcome to come here to vote, but I asked you not to talk about politics," my mom said. Her voice softened. "Please, Lauren, why do you always have to start a fight?"

I threw up my hands. "Whatever," I muttered. "He's gonna lose."

Looking back at the 2016 election is like watching a horror film. I want to scream, "Behind you!" at my past self, plodding along as if we were still on that march toward progress. I still haven't totally gotten over how convinced I was by the illusion of democracy as a historical achievement. The misconception persisted until near midnight on November 8, 2016.

My memory of the Before Times is most clearly encapsulated in that awful cake of Trump's face being carted around on election night. I remember it in shocking detail: it was a truly grotesque confection, including no less than four lines of wrinkles beneath each too-blue eye. "What a joke," I thought. How tragic this bust of icing would seem the moment he conceded—the profundity of his national humiliation cast in sugar and butter! I imagined Jared Kushner's voice sputtering for an aide to "get that thing out of here." I reveled in the absurdity of a bigoted reality star presuming he might win the presidency.

That night, we attempted small talk over dinner. Soon enough, we were done loading the dishwasher, and my dad deemed it a reasonable hour to start following the results. My mom couldn't understand why I had been itching to turn the TV on all night.

"I can wait until the morning," she said as I grabbed the remote. She was heading upstairs to bed, wrapped in that blanket every suburban mom hangs over the living room couch. It's possible I muttered back a "good night" without turning away from the TV. I was hunched over, making a snack out of my cuticles. My dad sat in silence. He wasn't sure what to do with himself. "They still haven't called California," he offered after one particularly melodramatic sigh. I wanted to scream, to ask why he was reassuring me of the outcome he had voted against mere hours ago, but Jersey was already blue, so I tried to drown my resentment with a gulp from my overfilled glass of red wine.

Nail-biting turned to crying by the time Pennsylvania was announced, and soon enough, it was official: Donald Trump was going to be the next president of the United States. Suddenly, the space between me and my father was an unbearable emotional gulf filled with throw pillows from Pier 1 Imports. I can still picture it: my hair piled in a messy bun, mascara streaming down my face, and my father wishing he had snuck off to bed two hours earlier with my mother, who had managed to avoid this mess entirely.

Across from him sat both his daughter and yet another "bleeding-heart liberal." The dad part of him won out.

"What are you so upset about?" he asked, in what I knew was a fumbled attempt to comfort me. They were the wrong words but I recognized that he was trying to talk about politics. He was searching for something to say. The silence stretched so long I thought he had given up, and then: "It's not going to go back to the 1950s."

"Is that really what you think I'm upset about?" I snapped. He stared at me. He seemed to understand that Trump was an embarrassment but couldn't fathom that he would have any impact on his life or his daughter's life.

I glared at him and got up to go to bed. "Good night," he called after me, as if it would all be okay in the morning.

It was clear that Trump was a hateful clown from the moment he announced his campaign by declaring that Mexicans are rapists. His bid for the presidency should have become unviable when we heard him brag about "grabbing [women] by the pussy" on tapes recorded by *Access Hollywood*. There ought to have been no question that the man who entered the political arena to challenge the birthright of our first black president was too racist to be allowed within twenty-five miles of the White House. There were CVS-length receipts for the case that this demonic sweet potato would be a menace in power, so for many, myself included, his win was unimaginable.

The next morning there were two sweet seconds before I realized it hadn't been a nightmare: Donald Trump had won the presidential election. It was as if a switch had flipped. It's hard to explain how I understood the world before, like trying to recapture the delight of peekaboo after developing object permanence. All at once, everything changed.

Part of the problem was that I had the privilege to view

American democracy as a historical achievement. It was a fore-gone conclusion that the system of checks and balances would protect our freedoms from fascism as our country ground along toward progress—sort of like a magical, self-cleaning litter box. On the horizon was one big equality rainbow, and then, record scratch, freeze frame: Donald Trump became our forty-fifth president.

On November 9, 2016, across the country American citizens, and especially young people, woke up to the true nature of the world we thought we were living in—and we had no choice but to do something about it. Trump's election made the country spark like an aurora borealis of light-bulb moments. Political awakenings involve a series of intellectual and emotional realizations that render inaction impossible; they can happen for any number of reasons, but rarely does such a huge portion of the population question the status quo. It's no coincidence that the term "woke," which refers to recognizing systemic injustice beyond individual tragedy, especially in regard to racism, has reached critical mass in popular culture. A huge portion of the country is awake now, and we're talking about politics more than ever before.

These sorts of epiphanies can spring from all sorts of inciting incidents. But the day after Trump won the election marked what may well be the most widespread series of political awakenings in recent American history.

Our political awakening can be attributed to a paradigmatic shift in the collective understanding of democracy and our role in the system. Trump's win shook many Americans out of a coma, as we were reminded that government by and for the people requires our input. It forced us to protest, march, run; to insist on raising our voices in ways that once seemed impossible. It forced us to ask who is in charge. Because if Donald Trump can become president, you really have to wonder who the hell makes the rules.

CHAPTER 1

POLITICAL AWAKENING

My political awakening was also literal. I opened my eyes the morning after the election and thought, "Holy shit, I have to do something about this." I'm a writer, so I wrote. More specifically, I'm a journalist, so I began to research and report. Before Trump won, my writing was often lowercase "p" political in the sense that it dealt in cultural power hierarchies, but I never thought I would write about traditional politics. The day after the election, it was no longer possible to write about anything else.

It was clear to me that lasting change would start with young people who felt the same way I did. I put a call out on Twitter, looking to interview young people who had undergone a political awakening in response to Trump's election. I expected to get maybe fifty responses total. I received more than three hundred and fifty emails within twenty-four hours, many including impassioned essays detailing the profundity with which everything had changed. I continued to hear these testimonies long after the election as I traveled the country, speaking to more and more young people in the midst of their political awakenings.

Details differed, but the central question remained the same.

Across my interviews, the newly awakened were asking, "Who makes the rules?" No longer were they willing to accept the unquestioned authority of politicans and media gatekeepers. The result was a stunning new sense of agency. Young people were rethinking their approach to civic participation, insisting on personal responsibility. (This should happen continuously in government supposedly by and for the people.)

Many of the young people I spoke to felt overwhelmed. "I felt a sense of hopelessness and that the problems were too big to change," a twenty-eight-year-old named Andrew wrote to me, identifying himself as the son of a Mexican immigrant living in Chicago. "I still felt that things might not pan out if we tried to organize for change," he said, "but if we didn't we're all well and truly fucked."

In one of my earliest interviews, a recently graduated political science major said it was only after Trump won that she saw that she could have a role in government. "I know it sounds stupid," she told me over the phone, "but I guess I thought of politics as a thing that important men did off in a room somewhere." One engineering PhD student was similarly baffled by his own passivity. "I understood that citizens could be attending town halls," he said, "but I never understood that I should be doing that." (By the time of our call, he had gone a step further and begun working as a labor activist on campus.)

This experience was eerily similar across accounts. Most of my interviewees sounded like people who saw the light and decided not to be assholes anymore. Time and again, I heard these five words: "I had no other choice."

"I genuinely never cared much for politics," a Temple University student named Monica told me. "Upon hearing the results of election night, I knew I had to educate myself to be able to support my opinions and express my views."

Seeking out information was the first step. But there was more to do. "Before 2016, I thought I was politically engaged because I had a subscription to the *New York Times* and would skim a couple articles every week," said a Case Western Reserve University student named Rachel. "I had never called to voice an opinion to my representatives, nor could I have even told you what their names were." After the election, she became a field organizer for Organizing for Action, a political group in Ohio. "I'd never contacted any of my members of Congress, rallied, protested, etc.," echoed a then twenty-nine-year-old named Stephen, who was raised in a conservative Southern home. "I've now done all of those, as well as challenged friends and family both online and face-to-face."

Across this wide range of experiences, there was consensus on what had changed, too. Before, caring about politics seemed like a secret club, coded in respectability and expertise. You had to have a particular set of qualifications, and, ideally, multiple pairs of boat shoes. Politics was something "important men did off in a room somewhere." Now, armed with knowledge, young people began to speak out on the issues that mattered most to them. They joined marches and protests, regularly contacted elected officials, volunteered for local candidates, and took action in other ways they'd never considered possible before. Some started nonprofit organizations or decided to run for office themselves.

I suspected this paradigmatic shift carried historic potential for a re-democratizing revolution. Even in its earliest stages, it was clear this moment was about more than the results of the 2016 election. Trump was just the allegedly-243-pound straw that broke the camel's back.

"WE ARE THE ONES WE HAVE BEEN WAITING FOR"

For example, on November 9, 2016, that switch flipped for Heather Ward, Rebecca Davis, and Kat Calvin. All three experienced the literal day-after awakening moment and radically altered their approach to civic participation as a result. Heather decided to run for office. Rebecca started a local activist group. Kat quit her job to start a nonprofit. All of that was stuff they'd thought about doing, but they hadn't felt the same sense of agency before.

Heather first thought about running for the school board when she was still covering it as the editor-in-chief of her school newspaper. In writing about the proceedings, she was struck by how out of touch the appointees seemed to be with the day-to-day lives of students. There were lawyers and a few wealthy moms but no one who might provide this crucial perspective. The purpose of the school board was to govern student life, and yet there was zero representation of the governed. Heather thought she might run for one of the volunteer positions someday. She filed the idea in her "eventually" folder. She wasn't qualified yet, she thought. One day she might be.

Heather was successful throughout her college career at Villanova. She studied hard while earning her accounting degree and received stellar grades. She was one of those kids who had her first job lined up by sophomore year. For Heather, it was a spot at Ernst & Young. She had few concrete plans beyond filling the position on November 8, 2016, right before everything changed.

On the day of the 2016 election, Heather was studying abroad in Milan. She'd been following the campaigns closely and intended to watch the results despite the time difference. Before going to bed, she set alarms for two a.m. and six a.m. She wanted to catch both the results and Hillary's victory speech. This was a historic moment, after all. America was about to elect its first female president. At two a.m., when Heather woke to news that Trump was in the lead, she promptly went back to bed, assuming it must be some kind of fluke. A few hours later, when she discovered that he had won, it felt like a bad dream—and only partly because she was still half-asleep.

The next day, Heather walked around Milan crying. "I don't know if any of my Italian friends had any idea what was going on," Heather explained later. She called her younger sister, back home in Pennsylvania, who reported that kids at the high school were crying, too. Heather was trying to make sense of what had happened herself, though she couldn't help but wonder what all those kids at school were feeling. That was precisely when she decided she was going to run for the school board. If not her, who? And if not now, when?

"I thought, 'Okay, that's it,'" Heather said. Heather is soft-spoken, with a mass of frizzy brown curls. She seems like the prototypical shy girl, but I caught the bite in her words. "I still didn't think I would win," she told me. "But I had to run."

Heather officially announced her decision in January of 2017, and in February connected with Run for Something, a nonprofit organization that works with progressive candidates on downballot elections. Even with that support, Heather wasn't convinced that she would win, but she threw herself into her campaign, knocking on more than fifteen hundred doors and making hundreds of phone calls. A host of enthusiastic volunteers did the same on her behalf. The primaries came during finals week at Villanova, so she slept approximately two hours a night taking her candidacy and college career to the finish line in tandem. Throughout the campaign, she was targeted aggressively by her opponent and remains vaguely unnerved by the adversarial strategy of a school board campaign. "Hold on," she said, flipping through the photos on her phone to show me an example. My phone buzzed to reveal an image of a poster calling her both "too inexperienced" and "too political," in bold capital letters.

I asked why she endured all that—the attacks, in particular— if she didn't think she was going to win. "I just thought a student had to try and run," she said.

After lunch, she texted an addendum to our interview. "Hey!" she wrote. "Probably unimportant but you had me thinking about why I worked so hard if I thought I was going to lose and I realized it was because I didn't want to let people down." The only choice was to try.

Either way, there was no going back to the way it was.

On November 9, 2016, while Heather was in Milan, Rebecca Davis was in New York City, thinking about how she didn't want to let people down. But unlike Heather, Rebecca wasn't crying alone on the street. People were crying alongside her.

Rebecca took the subway to work that day. She remembers that, instead of actively avoiding eye contact, commuters shared in collective grief. Rebecca couldn't stand it. She wanted to do something about what had happened. She couldn't think of what, exactly, so she texted a few friends, asking them to come over that night. The whole city was behaving as if someone had died, so she figured her gathering would be a lot like sitting shiva. She picked up too many bottles of wine and prepared to mourn in good company, until her guests started to show up. And then something unexpected happened.

She didn't realize it before the 2016 election, but Rebecca knew more about politics than most of her social circle. She had canvased, phone-banked, and volunteered for campaigns, and, for some people who came over, that made her their only friend who had ever engaged in political activism. Rebecca had been hoping to find someone to give her marching orders. She looked to Planned Parenthood and the American Civil Liberties Union at work that day, but both organizations seemed to be scrambling to respond. Now Rebecca had a room full of people who wanted her to tell them what to do next. She knew she needed to capitalize on that responsibility. "I had to do something then and there," Rebecca told me. "If someone didn't capture them in that very small window of opportunity right then, it would be lost and they would go back to what they were doing."

Many New Yorkers opposed Trump. Still Rebecca had long been bothered by the fact that New York isn't as progressive as its inhabitants may think. Upon further research, she discovered things were even worse than she'd imagined. "Did you know that abortion is considered unconstitutional in New York?" When we first spoke, Rebecca explained that abortion was technically a crime according to New York State law. (New York legalized abortion three years before *Roe*, but retained abortion in its criminal code, rendering abortion a crime with major exceptions.) I could easily imagine Rebecca unpacking this at her November 9 gathering. Her friends were grappling with a setback in 2016, unaware they had long been governed by a law passed in 1970. That was something Rebecca could try to fix.

Challenging the results of the presidential election felt impossible, but working to pass the Reproductive Health Act in New York was in the realm of possibility. The legislation was easy to explain and easy to understand—and Rebecca knew that was crucial for enlisting her friends. That night, Rebecca conceived of a project that would go on to be called Rally+Rise. In the months that followed, she devoted herself to launching the nonprofit, which aims to make politics accessible to those usually left out of the conversation, especially young women. She crafted a website, which has the aesthetics of a funky enamel pin from Forever 21, written in the voice of a friendly DM. "Rally+Rise is a grassroots group committed to making New York a progressive haven—all while redefining what it means to be an activist," the homepage reads. "And yes, you're def invited to join us."

One of the people who decided to join Rebecca was Alessandra Biaggi. Alessandra had heard whispers about antiquated reproductive laws in New York, but in speaking to Rebecca she was struck by the severity of the issue. That was part of what inspired her to run for the New York State Senate. Alessandra was Deputy National Operations Director for Hillary Clinton. The results of the election pushed her to run for office herself. At thirty-two years old, she joined a group of insurgent candidates in the state, and resolved to challenge long-term incumbent Jeff Klein, who *The Cut* called "New York's worst Democrat." He raised more than $3 million in an attempt to defeat her, and lost. Less than a month after she was inaugurated, Alessandra joined a group of newly elected insurgent Democrats who passed the Reproductive Health Act, and it all began with Rebecca's spinning into action the day after Trump's win.

On November 9, 2016, in LA, on the other side of the country, Kat Calvin was—like Heather and Rebecca—thinking about how she didn't want to let people down. Where Heather had been simmering over the lack of representation on the school board and Rebecca had been wondering about the backward New York senate, Kat had spent the past several years concerned about voter suppression.

In 2013, Kat followed the overturn of *Shelby County v. Holder*, in which the Supreme Court struck down section 4 of the 1965 Voting Rights Act, effectively gutting its protections. The ruling allowed widespread voter suppression and discrimination at the polls. Kat was devastated by the results of the case when the ruling was first issued, but she assumed the Democratic Party would take the initiative to find a solution. That didn't happen in 2014 or 2015, and in 2016, when Trump was elected, Kat determined that if someone was going to do something about voter suppression, it would have to be her.

A few months later, she traveled to Atlanta, Georgia, to launch the organization that would be called Spread the Vote. Kat hadn't been sitting things out before. She had worked as an activist in the past, and on the day of the election, she was working for a voter protection organization in Las Vegas. But after Trump's win, Kat was livid. She responded by changing absolutely everything about her life.

Kat knew she was diving headfirst into a new chapter as she packed up the things in her sun-flooded home on the West Coast, but she couldn't have had any idea of the extent to which voter suppression was boxing out the public in a government supposedly by and for the people.

After just a few weeks on the job, Kat learned that a government ID is necessary not only for voting but for basic survival. Some shelters refuse to accept people without a government ID; some food banks do the same. Requirements differ from state to state, but there is so much paperwork to complete to get a government ID, and fees, too. "Did you know you need a birth certificate to get an ID and an ID to get a birth certificate?" she asked me. I didn't.

Kat shared dozens of stories, each more confounding than the last. Perhaps the most upsetting was the account of a homeless man for whom she raised $630 for a secure government ID. He'd received heaps of fines for things like sleeping on a park bench and couldn't get a government ID without paying them off. That stuck with me: he had nothing, and yet he was supposed to pay several hundred dollars to participate in our democracy.

When Kat launched Spread the Vote, she understood government IDs allowed citizens to vote, but what she didn't know was that they also allowed people access to their citizenship. As she put it, "I wanted to help people vote, and it turns out they are being denied things way more fundamental than access to the ballot. They look at me and say, 'Sure, I'll vote, but I have to eat first.'"

Now Spread the Vote is active in Florida, Georgia, Indiana, Louisiana, North Carolina, Tennessee, Texas, Virginia, and West Virginia, with plans to continue growing. Along with her team, Kat has obtained IDs for hundreds of thousands of people, previously rendered invisible by the government created to serve them. If Trump hadn't won, she might still be in LA, hoping the Democratic Party would do something.

These are just a few examples. As I listened to these stories, and others, I understood that Heather, Rebecca, and Kat had been waiting for their turn or assuming someone else would take up the mantle eventually. Then Donald Trump became president, and they were rocked by a realization, one that the poet and activist June Jordan translated into the sublime: "We are the ones we have been waiting for."

Like Heather, Rebecca, and Kat, my political awakening forever altered my life, but only some of it was intentional.

"DONALD TRUMP IS GASLIGHTING AMERICA"

Before Trump's election, I was only half joking when I told my friends I wanted to be a pop culture anthropologist. I worked as an entertainment reporter at the *Huffington Post* before going freelance. (Some of the pieces I was proudest of included a dissection of what liminal adulthood looks like on-screen for the woman-child as opposed to the man-child, a deep dive on the way *The Rocky Horror Picture Show* has offered up a space for outsiders, and a profile of DJ Pauly D.) I often think about what my life would be like under a Hillary presidency. My pores would be smaller, maybe I'd have a yoga teacher certification, and I'd be parsing some cultural phenomenon with the dispassionate interest of a scientist peering through a microscope.

In the fall of 2016, I had started working on a piece about the commodification of sleep. I wanted to explore the way our need for rest is being turned into a product to be bought and sold. To that end, I interviewed William Dement, the psychologist who is largely recognized as the foremost researcher of the topic, about how much rest we actually need and why we never seem to get enough of it. But when I got back to my apartment the night after the election, I crumpled up the notes from our call. Now that I was awake, it seemed absurd to be writing about sleep.

As a journalist, it seemed to me that the most pressing item of concern was Trump's war on the truth. His cruelty toward the marginalized and his shameless authoritarianism made for a cornucopia of dystopian concern, but it would be impossible to combat any of it if the American public couldn't be certain whether what he said was true. Over the course of two days, fueled by a steady diet of coffee and wine, I wrote a book proposal attempting to grapple with the factors that brought us to the 2016 election. The sample chapter was an essay titled "Donald Trump Is Gaslighting America."

"Gaslighting" is a psychological abuse tactic in which victims are made to doubt their own sanity, and that, I argued, was exactly what Trump was doing to the electorate. I saw a chance to unpack his strategy of disinformation. If we recognized this method and understood how it worked, it would be easier to combat.

Trump spent his campaign undermining his own statements, sending aides out to contradict one another—lying over and over again, and then lying about ever having lied in the first place. The goal of this tactic was not so much to deceive as to confuse. Every time Trump opened his mouth, he issued a different version of the truth. It quickly became so hard to keep track of the deceptions and corrections, it seemed easier to give up entirely. With this method, Trump attempted to make the American people lose our grasp on reality. I saw Trump's gaslighting as a fundamental attack on democracy. It all comes down to this: without the truth, we have no foundation from which to resist.

At the time, I was working as *Teen Vogue*'s weekend editor. I'd accepted the job because the site took young women seriously. National and political news were covered with the same fervor as the latest in fashion and entertainment. I was working the weekend the Pulse terror attack claimed forty-nine lives.

We covered the shooting like a breaking news desk, and also frequently published updates regarding the content of Kylie Jenner's Snapchat.

I was working the Saturday in December after news broke that Trump contradicted the CIA's report on Russian election interference. It was far from the first time the incoming administration had lied to the American people, but his statement on the matter marked an objectively egregious act of deception. Trump had been dishonest throughout his campaign, but now that he was president-elect, his words bore the seal of the White House, escalating his statements to state-issued disinformation. I sent the essay to *Teen Vogue*'s digital editorial director, Phillip Picardi. We introduced it with the news of Trump's comments and clicked publish. My life has never been the same.

The essay went viral. I thought that maybe I'd had a few pieces go viral before, but this was something else entirely. Going viral is a lot like a first orgasm (when you know, you know). The sheer magnitude of reactions hit me like a tidal wave. My notifications couldn't load fast enough. Close to a million people read that post in under twenty-four hours, and apparently one of them was Dan Rather. I watched the reactions flow in from my standing desk, logging them like the captain of a space station. "Control, we have a Facebook post from the legendary newsman Dan Rather," I said aloud in my best walkie-talkie voice. "I repeat, a Facebook post from Dan Rather. Over."

The article cemented the idea of gaslighting in terms of the Trump administration's use of disinformation, but it also started a conversation about *Teen Vogue*'s audience. There was quite a bit of stealthy patronization in reaction to the piece. "*Teen Vogue*'s 'weekend editor,' whose last piece was on Selena Gomez's makeup, ably rips Trump. Thanks!" tweeted journalist and environmentalist Bill McKibben. "Did not expect this exegesis of gaslighting and its relationship to current day politics from *Teen Vogue*," wrote NPR media correspondent David Folkenflik. As the writer, professor, and editor Roxane Gay put it, "The condescension and surprise directed toward @TeenVogue for publishing great writers is a measure of how women/girls are underestimated."

I didn't think much of publishing the piece on *Teen Vogue*. Other pressing news that Saturday included Neville Longbottom's getting engaged, a viral video of some kid freaking out about animals in zoology class, and a Selena Gomez Pantene ad, which was newsworthy on account of her extremely cute makeup look. Apparently, mainstream media found it revelatory to juxtapose serious and nonserious interests.

I witnessed a stunning example of this a few weeks after I published the essay, when I was invited to appear on Fox News opposite Tucker Carlson. At the end of a hostile, antijournalistic segment, he questioned my right to participate in the political conversation, invoking entertainment and fashion articles I had published to *Teen Vogue*. Referencing a post regarding Ariana Grande's shoes, he told me, "Stick to the thigh-high boots, you're better at that."

It was the most shocking iteration of a thing I'd seen many times before. Even some positive reactions to the essay housed a kind of cavemanish attempt to bang the concepts of "young women" and "politics" together like rocks. Months later, on a *Today* show special about the success of *Teen Vogue*, the host was beaming as she asked me, "Do you like politics?"

I cringed but managed a smile. "Of course."

"Do you like thigh-high boots?"

"I do."

"Are they mutually exclusive?"

"They are not," I told her. I continued smiling despite feeling like I was on some ill-fated mash-up of *The Twilight Zone* and *Sesame Street*.

It became obvious to me, in a way I had never seen before, that the things young women like are wielded as disqualifiers of intelligence—especially when it comes to politics. It's based on the hierarchy of white supremacist patriarchy. Your participation in the political conversation is rejected with increasing levels of aggression depending on however many standard deviations you are away from being an old white dude, and it's a bunch of made-up nonsense.

Young women have plenty of nonserious interests, and so does everyone else. That doesn't mean we can't talk about politics. Although, to many, apparently that idea was shocking, and not only in regard to gender.

After I appeared on Fox, I was catapulted into the spotlight. I waited patiently for the insanity to die down, until it occurred to me I had to get used to it. As a friend once put it, "It's like you decided to write about politics, and a volcano opened in the center of the Earth."

Because "Gaslighting" was published on *Teen Vogue*, I became a sort of informal youth ambassador. I was routinely interrogated as to why young people aren't more involved in our government, why our voter turnout tends to be so low. On a daily basis, people asked that same question, over and over: Do young people really care about politics?

It didn't seem to me as if it was a matter of "caring." Certainly, I hadn't been apathetic before, but I was perplexed as to how I had done so little in the 2016 election. I was being asked to answer for an entire demographic as I pondered how exactly the shift had occured for me. With each interrogation, I imagined myself as a scandalized figure in a Lifetime movie, swarmed by reporters as I tried to leave the house. "Ms. Duca, how did you develop the confidence to express strong political opinions?" they might ask. "Please, Ms. Duca, how do we get young people to vote?"

In various iterations, I was being asked to respond to the same question. Here it is, once more: Do young people really care about politics? It's a ridiculous question—because of course we care. But as I tried to answer it for the talking heads and anyone else who asked, and as I continued to research and report and ask people like Heather, Rebecca, and Kat to tell their stories, I thought up a better one:

How will young people change American politics?

Young people didn't "suddenly care" about politics. Our interests and concerns didn't materialize out of thin air. The 2016 election was a wake-up call that translated our passion into action.

After my political awakening moment, I spoke to hundreds of young people. I asked them questions and listened to their stories of how they understood democracy before and after. I dug for clues in foundational texts, civic education programs, historical trends, and current generational surveys, trying to articulate the transformation unfolding in young people's approach to politics—and my own. On some level, my work was driven by a desire to articulate my own awakening moment.

We are asking who makes the rules in our democracy and demanding a role within it.

This moment offers a rare opportunity to rethink America's approach to civic participation. It will become a movement as the youngest generations challenge authority and insist on a place in the political conversation. We are no longer waiting our turn. A government by and for the people requires our voices, and we are finally demanding a role within it. We are demanding democracy for real.

What follows is a diagnosis of how we got here and a prognosis for moving forward. In the aftermath of this widespread political awakening, young people hold the power to change everything for good.

CHAPTER 2

PRACTICAL CITIZENSHIP

At the core of my awakening moment was the realization that our democracy is, in fact, not a magical, self-cleaning litter box. I thought I understood how it worked before the 2016 election. But I didn't comprehend the necessity of constant participation. This disconnect echoed out across my interviews. Most of the young people I spoke to could define what a democracy was, if asked, but could not describe its concrete application. As that one PhD student put it, "I understood that citizens could be attending town halls, but I never understood that I should be doing that."

Given the typical results of Jimmy Kimmel's man-on-the-street segments, it may be helpful to clearly define the term "democracy." Democracy refers to a power structure controlled by the majority. It can be direct, in which the people vote on each issue, or indirect, in which citizens elect officials to make decisions on their behalf (a process called representative democracy, which can also be referred to as a republic). It is never a finished product. Democracy is a dynamic process requiring daily maintenance. It is a thing we have, but it is also a thing we must do, and often. It requires continuous effort—well beyond voting. That can mean attending town halls, contacting elected officials, volunteering for campaigns, running for office, demonstrating, marching, protesting, organizing a boycott, spearheading voter outreach, and several thousand other activities. Practical citizenship looks different depending on who you are and what you care about. The point is that it's work, and we have to get into the habit of doing it all the time.

Instead, we tend to think of democracy as a perfect, finished product to be celebrated every year on the Fourth of July. Except, the American project was always intended to be an ongoing process, and the reality is that far too many of us have opted out. For us to have government by the majority, the majority must be civically engaged. Some of us vote, but few participate—that is, many Americans don't put forth the routine effort of practical citizenship. Instead, we tend to be satiated by a cheap brand of patriotism that regards democracy as a historical achievement.

Democracy is the basis of American pride. The supposed righteousness of our government system is the crown jewel in our exceptionalist complex, a diamond Rolex dripping out of the mouth of a Precious Moments ceramic eagle. We wave our flags with that uniquely American brand of patriotism, the most aggressive among us turning as bright red as a pre-barbecue burger when anyone dares to question the way we do things here. Our moral superiority derives from the essential ethical truth that democracy is the only legitimate form of governance. The problem is, that's not the system that currently exists in this country.

Here's another definition: *"Oligarchy." Noun. A power struc-ture controlled by a small number of people.* We elect officials to office, but in a functioning democracy, representatives must be accountable to their constituents, and that is blatantly not the case.

This is the sickness ailing American politics: without the habit of democracy, the people have no actual power. We have to actively engage with the political questions that define our lives, debating policy, demanding accountability for the elected officials who make the rules, and demanding a voice in the pro-cess, or our freedom is but an illusion.

Broadly speaking, Americans have a raging hard-on for how free we think we are. We recite Francis Scott Key's words, penned in 1814 and enshrined in our national anthem in 1931: this is "the land of the free and the home of the brave." Or there's Lee Greenwood's more recent iteration, "God Bless the U.S.A.," which declares freedom as our essential state of being: "I'm proud to be an American, where at least I know I'm free." There are, of course, countless more examples, but suffice it to say, you'd struggle to meet a seven-year-old who couldn't tell you in a sassy and self-satisfied tone, "This is a free country, last I checked."

It's all pageantry and no substance. There is endless empha-sis on our supposed liberty but little reflection on the genuine exercise of it and almost no understanding whatsoever of the duties associated with upholding our democracy. Or, as Thomas Paine once wrote, "Those who expect to reap the blessings of freedom must, like men, undergo the fatigues of supporting it." Translated into less flowery language: the idea that we will maintain our rights without upholding our responsibility is completely fucked.

THE MYTH OF AMERICAN PATRIOTISM

We can discern a lot of what we value as a culture from the stories we tell about our country, and especially the things that are taught in school. Not to go all "Santa Claus isn't real" here, but, like, let's be clear: you realize most of the mainstream historical narrative is bullshit, right?

National pride stems from a shared identity. Given that the American government was built from scratch on stolen land, our earliest governors made one up. In order to write a cohesive American story, they cooked up the Fourth of July, and later, Thanksgiving, to reinforce the synthesized narrative from Plymouth Rock to the Revolutionary War. Our unsettling origins of displacing people or bringing them here by force as slaves was SparkNoted as national accomplishments through a series of holidays, each complete with its own side dishes. Crafting American patriotism seemed to be an effort to entrance masses, not entirely unlike whatever combination of focus groups and algorithms have given us the *Transformers* franchise.

The effort of crafting a shared identity was formally enacted through the education system. In public schools, the goal was assimilation into nationalism. By the late 1800s, public school classrooms were engineered to create citizens who subscribed to unquestioning American pride. The idea was to Americanize the country into a "melting pot." This often was more than a figure of speech: in an image published by *Puck* magazine in 1889, a woman in an American flag sarong stirs a mix of people in stereotypical cultural garb using a giant spoon labeled "equal rights." On one side of the pot, a man raises a flag and knife in protest. "The mortar of assimilation," reads the caption. "And the one element that won't mix." Rather than empowering students with the tools for democratic participation, schoolhouses enforced empty devotion to the abstract concept of freedom. And thus emerged a concept of citizenship with approximately the nutritional value of a fried Oreo.

At the National Museum of American History in Washington, DC, there is a model of a schoolhouse desk alongside pictures of our earliest classrooms and a cue card encouraging visitors to critically observe the display. "How many flags and eagles can you find?" it asks. "Why were there so many?" I don't think that these are the kinds of questions we should be asking.

Andrew Lorenz has asked some of the questions we should. He wrote to me after the 2016 election, when he was a high school senior in upstate New York. His life in a conservative suburb was enshrined in all kinds of apple-pie privilege. He is a straight white dude from a wealthy family who was also the quarterback of the football team. He enjoyed the sort of high school experience I equated with a cartoon prom king, until he was physically shaken from his complacency. Tackled to the ground on the field and concussed, he blacked out. With that, Andrew's season was over, and so was his stock acceptance of his environment.

Watching from the sidelines to support his fellow players, he had a chance to really take in the proceedings without the distraction of being a star player. He watched the flags and the marching bands, suddenly seeing the ritual surrounding the game through fresh eyes. "I hadn't realized it before," Andrew told me. "The whole thing was a giant exercise in nationalism." It only took a head injury for him to see that clearly.

I was similarly shaken by the displays of shallow patriotism throughout my own high school experience. The flags and marching bands are the most visible manifestations of performative nationalism, but the most insidious ones happen in the classroom.

I didn't fully consider the way I learned American history until after my political awakening. That became especially painful during a trip to Hiroshima in January 2018. As my best friend and I walked into the city's Peace Memorial Museum, an older volunteer approached us. "Do you speak English?" he asked. "Would you like to know more about the history of this place?" We nodded yes, and he started at the beginning. On August 6, 1945, at 8:16 a.m. Japanese time, a bomb collapsed and burned everything within a two-kilometer radius of where it struck the city. At least eighty thousand people died in the immediate aftermath, though that staggering number doesn't account for all of the tens of thousands more who fell dead days, weeks, and months later, their bodies yielding to the radiation still simmering in their bloodstreams. There were statistics like these, and then more specific details, like skin falling off of bones and dropping to the ground, or the heat-conducting patterns of kimonos etched into backsides.

There was all of this incomprehensible suffering, and then, three days later, a second bomb dropped over Nagasaki, where historians estimate that more than seventy thousand people were killed. The US military flew over Hiroshima, surveyed the impact of the destruction, and then dropped a second bomb.

As we walked through the museum, there were personal stories spliced with the historical time line. The exhibit began with Albert Einstein's letter to FDR on the process of transforming uranium, which would lead to "extremely powerful bombs of a new type." This initiated the wildly expensive initiative known as the Manhattan Project, and it became clear to me that cost was the primary motivation for the dropping of the bomb. The US government framed the choice as a necessary step in ending the conflict. But they never warned the Japanese military. Instead, they simply devastated a country. It seemed to me that Hiroshima wasn't about enacting necessary force; it was about justifying the money spent on building a nuclear weapon no one needed. Tens of thousands of people died in what was essentially a public relations effort.

It's hard to explain the profundity of the shame I felt in learning all of this. I truly hadn't known. By the time we left the museum—hours later, because neither of us wanted to be the first to suggest it was time to go—the grief had shifted into anger. I thought about how I had been taught all of this in high school. There was no discussion of the lack of warning or the devastation that followed. Hiroshima was little more than a bullet point. I'm not sure Nagasaki was brought up at all.

The presiding American narrative often presents this country as a white-knight savior. The various atrocities perpetrated by the United States are swept out of view or reframed as victories. We are taught the big wins in the march of progress but none of the actual stuff of democracy. It's as if these critical turning points happened with the wave of a wand.

Perhaps the most obvious way to look at this is through the way we are taught about slavery. Why isn't there more emphasis on the lack of white people who opposed slavery in the average high school history class? The narrative zooms in on the heroes who saved the day. The country that values freedom above all else was built on the enslavement of an entire race, and public schools spend less time reflecting on that than fetishizing Abraham Lincoln's top hat. The focal point of the story is the freeing of the slaves, which conveniently deemphasizes the fact of how they came to be enslaved in the first place.

Another example is the fight for women's suffrage. In March 2018, I was assigned a review of four young adult books on women's history for the *New York Times*. Again, I was jarred by the things I did not know. In pages intended for children ages eight to twelve I found a more complex representation of female historical figures than anything I had encountered across my academic career. At first, this was a thrilling development. As I noted in the essay, I briefly became a dispenser of feminist fun facts: "'Did you know that Frederick Douglass spoke at the Seneca Falls Convention of 1848?' I asked a friend excitedly over happy hour. ('Yes,' he replied. 'But only because you already told me that last week.')"

But my initial giddiness hardened into cynicism. As I had

discovered in Hiroshima, my exposure to this massive chapter in US history had been reduced to a few sentences on a time line, framed as a progressive achievement, rather than the overdue righting of a wrong. It took almost one hundred years of struggle in order for half the population to earn the right to vote. There was a century of marching, organizing, petitioning, and protesting before women were acknowledged as *technically* human. We learn about women's earning the right to vote as a happily-ever-after moment. The profound history of democratic practice behind the achievement is conspicuously missing.

This is by design. Glossing over the origins of the ongoing fight for gender equality obscures the practical application of democracy. The fight for women's suffrage is one of the most significant examples of petitioning and protest as democratic practice. Skipping over a complete teaching of this subject matter is another way in which our indoctrination into the fraternity of patriotism takes precedence over our commitment to practical citizenship.

RIGHTS AND RESPONSIBILITIES

At the public school level, I suppose it only makes sense that the power of the state is not interested in teaching the practice of dissent. "Dissent" may seem like a strong word for how practical citizenship should be taught in public schools, but it's the right one. Dissent is a fundamental part of true democracy. In the relationship between the governors and the governed, no legitimate yes can exist without the power to say no. This is crucial: without consent of the governed, no legitimate goverment can exist, and government by and for the people is reduced to a slogan.

I never learned about this in high school. And it's the kind of civic education that would be most useful to us now.

Our founding fathers emphasized the necessity of teaching rights and responsibilities, most notably John Dewey, who called education the "midwife" of democracy. The argument for the necessity of this kind of civic education is quite simple. The Declaration of Independence clearly states that legitimate government requires the consent of the governed. That is the very basis of American democracy, and part and parcel of that idea is that citizens must be equipped to provide their consent.

It is a textbook catch-22 that civic education is required to reform this problem, the darkest twist of all being that its absence obscures the problem in the first place. If you don't have a civic education, how can you provide consent? If you don't have a civic education, how can we even have this conversation?

These are broad strokes. It's difficult to talk about the current state of civic education because the American education system is decentralized. What is required of public schools varies not only from state to state but from district to district. I looked to standardized testing to get a sense of the proficiencies of the average student's civic knowledge, or lack thereof. If only American public schools treated authoritarianism with the same seriousness awarded to the dangers of cigarettes.

In many cases, students are exposed to civic education but do not leave school prepared to engage in practical citizenship. Ninety percent of students take at least one civics class in high school, but only 25 percent score a "proficient" on the civic assessment test from the National Assessment of Educational Progress. The issue is not a lack of civic education but what is being taught, and, equally, if not more important, the way it is being taught.

To learn more, I spoke to Beth Rubin, a professor of educational theory at Rutgers University. Beth was a social studies teacher until, frustrated with the way things were done, she left her job to pursue a doctorate. Now she's working to overhaul the public school approach to civic education, partnering with teachers to implement what she calls "meaningful, relevant civic learning." "Democracy is not a done deal," Beth told me on the phone, explaining her methodology. "US civic life is constantly under debate, and the class should be a place where we're incorporating students as participants in that debate."

I also spoke to Beth's colleague Elizabeth Matto. Elizabeth is an associate research professor at the Eagleton Institute of Politics at Rutgers University and an advocate for teaching civic engagement who helped create the book on the topic. (Seriously, it's called *Teaching Civic Engagement Across the Disciplines*.) Matto's current work seeks to combat the lack of rigorous civic education standards by prescribing methods for teaching it alongside other subjects. She has found that many of the teachers she works with want to bring civic discourse into their classrooms but often feel underprepared by virtue of having been denied basic training in this area.

Civic education requires learning how to vote, but it's also about learning how to participate in the political conversation. Researchers Diana E. Hess and Paula McAvoy explore the best way to teach these skills in their 2014 book, *The Political Classroom*, which maps out a clear curriculum for the democratic practice of building consensus from debate. "Helping students develop their ability to deliberate political questions is an essential component of democratic education," they write in the introduction to the text. Ultimately, teaching civic education depends on empowering students to gather information, form opinions, and make political decisions based on facts. Democratic citizenship requires political agency—or, the sense that one has the ability to participate in the political conversation.

But often, even when they are given access to rudimentary civic teaching, students do not feel so empowered.

Here's an example: After the 2016 election, James Wellemeyer found himself pondering the gap between the theory and practice of democracy. Then a junior at Lawrenceville, a private boarding school in New Jersey, James was shocked by the low voter turnout rate among young people. According to the Pew Research Center, just 49.4 percent of millennials cast ballots in the 2016 election. James heard the excuses from his peers who had turned eighteen. They'd gotten busy, they hadn't bothered. He wondered how that was possible. Media coverage framed low youth turnout as an issue of apathy, but that didn't track for James. The halls of Lawrenceville had been buzzing with anticipation ahead of November 8. It wasn't that James's peers didn't care about politics—in fact, they seemed to care quite a bit, and yet the majority hadn't voted. He couldn't figure out why.

James started by talking to people. He sought out friends who hadn't gotten involved but quickly became more interested in those who had. He wanted to understand what propelled them into action. He had received a thorough education at Lawrenceville, but everything he'd learned about civic participation had been presented in the abstract. He was never shown that he could be involved in the political process as a young person—let alone how.

Part of what motivated James was a personal inquiry. He wanted to figure out why he hadn't been more active ahead of the 2016 election.

"I didn't volunteer on campaigns, because I didn't know I could," James told me. "I wasn't super involved, because I didn't really know how to get super involved."

That's when he realized the issue went well beyond voter turnout. Instead, it seemed to James as if his peers were waiting for their turn. Taking his interviews to university campuses, he found college students who said they wanted to do something in government, but only after pursuing another career first. One guy who was super into politics had decided that he had to work on Wall Street for a decade or so before he could get serious about pursuing elected office. That seemed irrational to James. "Although, I guess I can see where he got the idea," he said in retrospect. "Look at the people representing us. They're all much older."

"I never would have even thought to get engaged in politics when I was thirteen years old," he continued. "But I do think that thirteen-year-olds can get involved in politics."

In this, the issue with how young people understood democracy crystallized for James: there was a chasm between its definition and its application. Democracy is a thing you do, and young people need to see that in action. It makes a difference when the example is set by other young people.

A basic civic education outlining the nuts and bolts of US history and government wasn't the full answer. He'd had that himself, and he still felt alienated from the political conversation before the 2016 election. Instead, James thought, his peers needed to see young people engaged with politics. With the help of the competitive Welles Award grant from the Lawrenceville School, awarded to ten out of one hundred applicants, he made it his mission to do just that in the form of a civics textbook called *Young Voices*.

Over the course of the summer, James spoke to more than sixty politically active fourteen-to-twenty-two-year-olds and compiled their stories into one hundred and fifty pages of something sorely missing from the typical civic education: concrete examples of practical citizenship. Geared toward students ages ten to sixteen, the goal of *Young Voices* is to centralize youth narratives as a starting point for discussion, in order to more deeply engage students in politics.

Each chapter includes a "Youth Opinion" section, featuring the views and experiences of James's subjects, which are followed by discussion questions. Rather than being presented with the definitions of abstract ideological principles, students are given information about each topic and then hear from their peers. The first chapter after the introduction features forceful stances on US government from high school students. "I really think the Electoral College is outdated and obsolete because more Americans should not be voting for the losing candidate," a young delegate to the Democratic National Convention named Frederick Bell said. "Everyone's voice should be given equal weight." That section also includes a rejection of gerrymandering from a Youth Ambassador at the 2017 Women's March named Clara Nevins, who stated that redistricting is "a huge problem in this country," adding that "roughly 20 seats in Congress are simply decided by gerrymandering."

Later in *Young Voices*, a chapter on youth power centers around young people discussing the movements that inspired them. Devon Kurtz, who is identified earlier in the text as a student who helped fight the opioid crisis in his state, discusses how he was moved by the nonhierarchical structure of the Stonewall riots, which were protests for LGBTQ rights that you totally should have learned about in high school. "There wasn't the same power dynamic of a lot of movements where the older people in the movement have more power. Pretty much whoever was most active, most passionate, became a leader," he explained. Frederick's voice appeared again in regard to Michael Brown's death at the hands of police officers and the Ferguson protests that followed the tragedy in August 2014. "Young people got out there and said, 'This could happen to my friend' or 'This could happen to me,'" he told James. "I think that activism was very inspiring."

Each of these sections leads to discussion questions, asking students to contemplate what youth movements have in common or what they might change about the structure of the US government. That's what's special about Wellemeyer's work. Rather than instructing readers on the way things are, it encourages them to think for themselves. In other words, it teaches political agency.

GENERATION CITIZEN

The idea that you have the right to a voice is different than the experience of feeling empowered to speak up. Once you have the tools to express political opinions based on a foundation of information, practical citizenship is a matter of self-determination.

One of the most important expressions of practical citizenship is voting, but how it extends beyond that depends on your immediate circumstances: your neighborhood, the people around you, the things you care about, the things you think should be different. To internalize that understanding requires witnessing practical citizenship in action. I saw one of the most effective models of this at Generation Citizen, a nonprofit that is transforming the way civic engagement is taught by bringing the subject to life. The most exciting part? It only takes two college volunteers ten weeks to teach the program to middle and high school students. That model is very scalable—which is the business way of saying that with enough support and the right legislation, robust civic education could easily be the standard for public schools all over the country.

Founded in 2008 at Brown University, Generation Citizen is a 501(c)(3) nonprofit that plugs into a state's civics requirements with a lesson plan called "Action Civics," in which students enact direct change in their communities. Generation Citizen started in four classrooms in Providence and has since reached more than thirty thousand kids across six states. The curriculum is simple: students begin by debating local issues, in order to build consensus around a problem they'd like to solve; they research and analyze the causes; and then they develop a solution, which they put into action by meeting with legislators, building petitions, and crafting opinion pieces for local publications. In many cases, they see the direct results of their work informing policy, but, regardless of the success of their project, they come to understand practical citizenship far better than, well, the average American citizen.

All of this is implemented by "Democracy Coaches" who themselves undergo something of a transformation in the process. I spoke to a senior at Hunter College named April Snape, who said it was through Generation Citizen that she felt she had truly become "quote-unquote: woke" to the ways in which she might effect change.

As a Democracy Coach, April saw what was lacking in high school classes and felt it was mirrored in her college courses—despite her being a political science major. "It's one thing to have an instructor up there going 'blah, blah, blah,'" she said, giggling at her own impression of an out-of-touch professor. "It makes a difference to have a Democracy Coach, someone closer to these kids in age, someone who understands them and can convince them that they really can make a difference."

That was a lesson that April needed to learn herself. In fact, it's why she pursued the position. "In this political climate, I feel like a lot of young people don't know where they stand," she explained. "I kind of did it to understand how I could foster systemic change. At that time, I only thought of voting as my go-to, as far as politics and civic duties were concerned. I never saw people like me explaining how to be politically engaged."

Through her work as a Democracy Coach, April bridged the divide between a theoretical and a practical understanding of citizenship. "I'm a political science major, and my teachers talk about things in a theoretical approach," she continued. "But when I go into the classroom, I have to make it tangible for students to understand. I have to explain that this is something you can actually do. I think the hardest part is taking the theoretical approach away and making it something tangible, so that it's something that they can easily touch, and feel, and grasp."

While doing this, she also bridged the divide for a classroom of underprivileged high schoolers who needed to see someone like them doing the thing. "It was definitely a learning process for me," April said. "I think the students see that you're not there to dictate to them. The difference between a teacher and a Democracy Coach is that a Democracy Coach is someone who is close to you in age, who is also trying to find their way through the system."

I got to see April's and the other Democracy Coaches' work in action in the fall of 2017 during Civics Day at Riverside Church—a historic interdenominational house of worship, where Dr. Martin Luther King Jr. gave his famous Vietnam War Speech. The event was the culmination of the action civics lesson plan, described to me as "a science fair for civics." Instead of volcanoes oozing food-colored dishwashing detergent, there were proposals to limit "clout chasing" posts showcasing gang violence on social media, and a call for a more comprehensive sexual education program, inspired by the rise of #MeToo. Poster boards covered in construction paper and glitter glue concealed the rigor behind their displays: these presentations revealed a thoughtful methodology dedicated to improving communities, along with intricate plans for putting them into action, many of which had either begun in earnest or already proven successful. Students were communicating with their school's faculty in ways they had never imagined possible. They were in direct contact with local officials, turning grassroots energy into effective collective action as petitions supporting their proposals gathered steam.

I had volunteered to be a Civics Day judge. Rating the plans on criteria like "grassroots change" and "systemic impact" on a scale of one to four, I fought the urge to give perfect scores to projects focused on police-community relations, mass incarceration, school safety, and public monuments. The energy of the students was inspiring. It was as if they were supercharged by awareness of their personal efficacy.

"I used to think we couldn't do anything, because we're just students," a then–high school senior named Jewel told me. She'd heard I was a reporter and asked if I'd like to take a look at her work, tucked into the back corner of the auditorium. Now she was standing in front of her group's project along with her Democracy Coach and a teacher from her school, using the flashlight from her cell phone to direct my attention across her poster board. None of them could stop smiling.

When Generation Citizen began its work at her school, Jewel knew right away that their project should tackle the lack of support services for students. She explained that the six hundred students in her school had only a guidance counselor, college counselor, and social worker looking out for their mental health. Much of the time, the counselors' and social worker's days were consumed with mandated sessions, meaning that students in need often found themselves turned away, even when they were desperate for help.

"A lot of kids in this school are really struggling," she told me. That became undeniable when one student committed suicide. She'd spent months sleeping through class, and teachers had yelled at her to wake up or called her lazy. Only after she took her own life did it become clear that she had been severely depressed. She'd needed help, and there was no one who had the capability to see the warning signs.

Jewel also felt the effects of this firsthand. "I have a lot to deal with," she said. "Like, a lot." Suddenly, her pride in her project seemed to grow from defiance. She was taking aim at a world that had sought to crush her, refusing to take no as an answer. And there had been nos along the way.

The first solution was more guidance counselors, but the school's budget made that an impossibility. There just wasn't enough money. Other students in the class had suggested fundraising, but Jewel saw that their bake-sale efforts would be like digging around in a piggy bank to buy a laptop. There had to be another way.

Some teachers were tapped out, but many expressed interest

in students' lives. In her research, Jewel had discovered mental health education training for high school instructors, and it was there she saw the solution: What if every teacher in the school was armed with the skills of a guidance counselor? Then students could pick the authority figure they were most comfortable with in times of need. If nothing else, it would help prevent students from languishing through depressive episodes in isolation. To that end, Jewel targeted training programs that would arm teachers with the skills to recognize and discuss critical mental health issues. She assembled a proposal and a petition of support, and it worked: the next month, her principal had agreed to dedicate a day to mandatory professional development for all of the teachers in the school.

It was a more innovative and effective solution than even the school board would have been expected to develop, and it came from an eighteen-year-old who, months earlier, had felt totally powerless. Before she met her Democracy Coaches, Jewel said, she wouldn't have even thought she had a shot. "I would just give up," she said. "I would just not even try."

Jewel's project was uniquely impressive, but it showcased an essential shift. Regardless of how innovative any given project was, there was a clear transformation in how these kids understood their political agency. They emerged from the work totally convinced of their personal power to create real change.

In one particularly inspiring moment, a freshman named Izik spoke about how he had changed over the past ten weeks. He had started the training as one of the quietest kids in school and was now a class leader. Generation Citizen recognized his achievements, and that meant he had to prove it by taking the microphone before a room filled with his peers and hundreds of strangers on Civics Day. As he shuffled up to the stage, I heard someone yell, "Go, Izik!" and then whisper, "Yo, he used to be so shy."

Izik braced himself as he told a story of wanting to ask a question in class and not being able to summon the courage. "I was nervous, like I am to talk to this big crowd now," he read from his notes, growing louder, "but it was a big lesson learned. I learned to be confident and ask the questions I need to." The crowd went wild.

"Generation Citizen has inspired me, because I feel like I'm making a community . . . This project changed my perspective of politics"—he paused, turning the page—"a lot, because I was never really able to speak up for myself." His trembling voice steadied with each word. "I wouldn't say many things about the issues that were happening nowadays. I would just sit there and listen to everyone else. But not anymore," he continued. This time, when the audience cheered, I cheered with them.

Except this wasn't just about what Izik was able to accomplish on his own, and he made a point of acknowledging that. "Throughout our project, individual students have stepped up and made an impact on our work, but I didn't want to focus on the time that one student was making a difference. I feel like our class as a whole was doing so," Izik concluded. "We worked together on different tasks toward one larger goal, and together we took the steps to accomplish what we need to. We learned together, we grew together, we made a difference together."

There was another round of thunderous applause, and now it felt like the kids of Generation Citizen were also clapping for themselves.

I was stunned by how effective the work of Izik's Democracy Coaches had been, and relieved by the ease of it all. This thirteen-year-old bundle of nerves had not only found a stunning new sense of political agency, he had a more rigorous understanding of participatory democracy than most of the electorate. The process begins with the development of an individual voice—as happened somewhat literally in Izik's case—but as he well understood, more so than that, it was about building to the impact of collective power. That's what government by and for the people actually looks like.

Instead, most curriculums depict American governance as a historical achievement, mostly glossing over the genocide of indigenous people, slavery, suffrage, and government-perpetrated atrocities like the bombing of Hiroshima, ultimately emphasizing pride over participation. The obstruction of proper civic education is itself political.

For example, in 2012 the College Board introduced new guidelines for the Advanced Placement government course in order to better teach students how to think critically about the nation's founding narrative. One of the objectives of the new curriculum was to encourage students to "investigate how American foreign policies and military actions have affected the rest of the world." Three years later, the Republican National Committee complained that the new framework "emphasizes negative aspects of our nation's history," and Oklahoma state representative Dan Fisher introduced a bill to defund the program, because, he said, it teaches "what is bad about America."

One thing that is "bad about America" is that our lack of civic education is both a cause and effect of our lack of civic education. It's all linked, and inextricably so: changing the way civic education is taught in public schools could be achieved through the work of practical citizenship, if only that were taught. The Generation Citizen Democracy Coaches would tell you that if you don't like the history or civics curriculum in your local high school, find out who is behind it. Look to the school board and other elected positions in your area. Even just asking these questions, and gathering information, can jump-start the process of change.

This is but one of countless options for getting involved. Think of James, April, Jewel, or Izik. Zero in on an issue you care about and dive in headfirst. It can be almost anything, but choose something. Just know this: there are no rights without responsibilities, no government by and for the people without our input, no democracy without the constant, ongoing work of practical citizenship.

CHAPTER 3

THE POLITICAL-INDUSTRIAL COMPLEX

Many Americans are severely lacking in the knowledge required for participatory democracy, but the problem is more than a matter of comprehension. Even if you know your shit like Hermione the day before an exam, political agency often remains out of grasp. "There were a lot of things I wanted to change before," a sophomore at Colby College told me after I visited the school. "I didn't see how I could make any difference." In short, it all just seems so fucking impossible—we think we can't, and so we don't.

This attitude predates the 2016 election. Insofar as the health of the American project is concerned, Donald Trump is a huge red herring. As I spoke to more and more newly awakened young people, it became clear that Trump was just the symptom that made the disease impossible to ignore. I was still looking for the thing that made us sick in the first place.

So, I went back to the beginning. I read foundational texts and civics textbooks. I studied American political ideals and the way we are taught them.

ONE INDUSTRIAL COMPLEX TO RULE THEM ALL

A few months into my research, my notes were starting to resemble Carrie's strategy board from *Homeland*, only drawn with an embarrassingly extensive collection of rainbow gel pens. I had begun to feel like I was banging my fists on concrete when I found the term that clicked everything into place: "the political-industrial complex."

I first encountered the term in the pages of a Harvard Business School paper titled "Why Competition in the Politics Industry Is Failing America," in which authors Katherine M. Gehl and Michael E. Porter use the lens of business theory to argue that our current political system is a corrupt industry that presents the idea of solutions as an impossibility.

Reading those words was like the writerly equivalent of discovering Rumpelstiltskin's name. At first, I felt like an idiot for being unfamiliar with the term, and then I discovered that it has barely come up in political reporting at all. According to the paper where I discovered it, the term "political-industrial complex" had only appeared in three works prior: twice in academic journals in 2003 and 2005, and once in the *Wall Street Journal* in 1990. You may be familiar with the phrase "industrial complex," given that our society is riddled with them: the military-industrial complex, the charitable-industrial complex, the bridal-industrial complex, to name a few. An industrial complex is an informal alliance of industries that conspire to maintain or increase power, and this self-reinforcing ecosystem fuels the machine. The political-industrial complex is at the core of the whole systemic-corruption rat king—one industrial complex to rule them all.

I know that idea may seem intimidating—at least, that's how I felt when I first started reading an eighty-pager on business theory. But stay with me. As it stands, the United States is effectively an oligarchy: a small number of people control the levers of power that dictate the laws, norms, and values that govern American life. In order to overthrow that unjust hierarchy, we need to build individual action into collective power with the goal of regaining a voice for the American public as a collective. A huge part of the problem is that most of us don't feel like it's worth it to even bother. A self-fulfilling prophecy of inevitability arises from our acceptance of inefficacy in this regard. That sense of fatalism is most effectively understood as political alienation.

Political alienation, or the sense that one cannot effect change, is a direct result of the political-industrial complex, which allows the consolidation of power among the few to endlessly perpetuate itself. If we can give this thing a name, we can begin the work of defeating it. Just like Rumpelstiltskin.

Gehl and Porter define the political-industrial complex as "the interconnected set of entities that support the duopoly" formed by the Democratic and Republican Parties. These include special interests, lobbyists, consultants, and the media, among other players. In breaking down this ecosystem, these elite power brokers focus on competition between the two parties, denying the possibility for healthy debate, or anything beginning to resemble effective solutions for our political problems. Time and again, we are told that a stalemate between the two teams is "just the way things are."

Here's how the political-industrial complex works according to Gehl and Porter: Aware that head-to-head combat will lead to mutual destruction, Democrats and Republicans instead create artificial competition, differentiating themselves in the American mind as the only two viable choices in the marketplace. Together, they conspire to box out additional competitors as they compete against each other for the money needed to win elections. Rather than crafting public policy that reflects public will, they focus on campaign financing. It's all a big scam where each side tries to be nothing more than "the lesser of two evils." (This reasoning is often applied to the choice between Hillary Clinton and Donald Trump, though the comparison between the two is less apples to apples and more apples to radioactive sludge.) In focusing on artificial competition, the duopoly frames the lack of effective legislation as the result of the other guy's obstinacy. That means we get crappy, binary choices—and no solutions. Gehl and Porter argue that this is about not any one politician but the nature of the entire setup in which they operate. We tend to think of politics as a public institution but it is an industry, and one of the few in which the major players set their own rules without being held accountable to the majority of customers.

POLITICAL CUSTOMERS

The concept of "customers" in politics is especially helpful in understanding what's ailing our democracy. The people running the business of American politics make no effort to make their product appealing to the public—and then they blame us for our lack of interest. That's their responsibility, too. Not only do they shirk this democratic duty, they aggressively diminish the public's ability to participate (see also: Kat Calvin's work at Spread the Vote). The foremost concern of our elected officials ought to be ensuring a voice for their constituents, or anyway, that's what it would be if they gave a shit about democracy.

Probably the easiest way to see this concept in practice is the way the major political candidates—and especially incumbents—approach young people during campaigns, or rather, the fact that they usually don't.

To that end, I'd like to tell you a story about Al Gore. At the Teen Vogue Summit in the spring of 2018, Gore appeared onstage with the comedian Billy Eichner. Midway through their conversation, Eichner brought up the upcoming midterms, citing low turnout statistics—a 10 percent drop-off to 26 percent of all eligible voters under forty in the 2014 elections, according to Nonprofit VOTE. Armed with this statistic, Gore turned to the audience. Shifting in his seat to face the crowd of mostly high school and college students, he said, in that low Southern drawl of his, "You know that's pathetic, right?"

I had the opportunity to interview Gore after he got offstage. I waited for him in one of the basement classrooms of the New School, where the conference was hosted. He arrived flanked by two meticulously dressed young men who seemed like the kind of bodyguards you'd pick up at a J.Crew. One of them told me that I had five minutes.

Gore has been fighting for climate change awareness since he was a member of Congress in the 1970s. Even after four decades of work, there is not nearly enough urgency in that conversation. Under President Trump, we are faced with an Enviornmental Protection Agency that is undermining the findings of its own scientists and actively rolling back the few guidelines intended to reduce emissions. Indeed, man-made global warming was a crisis well before we were faced with an administration whose guiding policy position seems to be "Fuck the Earth."

But Gore is no longer an elected official. He can't influence politics in the same way he did when he was in office. Instead, he looks to the next generation—and is focused on encouraging young people to vote for smart environmental policy.

But he hasn't tailored his message to reach young people, nor does he express any need to use his platform to push current representatives to do so. "Why don't politicians do a better job at catering to young people?" I asked him.

Gore's answer was yet another catch-22: politicians will listen to young people if young people start showing up to vote. "These young people really can help change that pattern," he said. "If you start voting in large numbers, you better believe that people in both parties would be falling all over themselves to listen."

That logic is amazing to me. Millennials are now the largest demographic in the United States, and Gen Z is right behind. The youngest generations have the power to gain influence in terms of numbers alone if we raise our voices at the polls. That said, encouraging sustained political engagement is not as simple as nagging young people to "just vote already." Young people should vote, of course, but it is the responsibility of our elected officials to galvanize constituent participation. The problem is that the current political system does not incentivize politicians to cater to the people they represent. Most don't feel any need to sell their product to young people, effectively rejecting our status as political subjects by refusing to cater to us as political customers.

The Teen Vogue Summit makes for obvious context. The conference is designed to look, more or less, like Urban Outfitters. This aesthetic is easy to emulate. Assembling the stock crap that my generation is drawn to doesn't require a marketing genius. You get a potted plant, a neon sign, and a nice bold sans serif font, and, boom, you've got a subway ad for the latest disruptive millennial brand. If politicians wanted to get young people interested in politics, that stuff would be all over the place. Instead, campaigns have the approximate appeal of a dentist's office.

So it's startling when you see what the strategy of approaching voters as customers actually looks like. Then-thirty-four-year-old NYU business professor Suraj Patel's congressional campaign used it to run in the Twelfth District of New York. Suraj lost the Democratic primary in an unexpectedly close race against incumbent Carolyn Maloney, but his campaign design felt so fresh, I wondered if it wasn't the earliest seeds of an entirely new approach to politics. It made sense that he was running arm in arm with the eventual rock star of New York's Fourteenth

District, Alexandria Ocasio-Cortez. They were doing things differently, not following the political playbook—for Suraj that meant building a campaign that wasn't boring as hell.

It was a miserable winter day in February 2018 when I met Suraj and his chief creative officer, Anjelica Triola, at their headquarters. I assumed I was looking for an office building, that the entrance would include a ride up some relic of an elevator to cubicles and fluorescent lights. But when I arrived at the address, I looked up to see Suraj's smiling face beaming from a millennial-pink campaign sign plastered in the first-floor window of what was once the social justice bar Coup.

Then I saw the same smile beaming in 3-D form. Suraj had perfect white teeth and the kind of thick, lush hair you'd expect to see on the cover of a romance novel. "Do you know what this place used to be?" he asked, holding open the door, as I peeled off my puffer jacket. "It was this bar that would donate all proceeds to organizations like Planned Parenthood and the ACLU," he said, answering his own question before I could ask where to hang my coat.

"He wanted to do an event there," Anjelica said as she walked up to shake my hand. "And when we saw it was closed, we knew where our campaign headquarters were going to be."

I looked around. The room was lit by rustic sconces of the sort that would be overpriced at Anthropologie. Deep-blue couches were placed strategically near ceramic tile tables. Wine bottles filled the mirrored shelves of the bar. The walls were hung with progressive slogans, scrawled in graffiti-style typography. There was a display of clothing that might as well have been for sale at American Apparel. "Political Campaign" read one sweat-shirt in bold white letters. And then, along the arm, "Suraj Patel for Congress." I had been under the impression that campaign headquarters were meant to be soul-sucking office spaces bathed in unflattering lighting. By comparison, this may as well have been an Instagram installation.

The décor was only the most visible manifestation of Suraj's strategy.

You'll note that "chief creative officer" is not a typical cam-paign position. "No one has a head of creative," Anjelica said, explaining her role managing a team of writers, designers, and videographers. "Isn't that wild?"

Anjelica has a background in marketing and felt that basic promotional techniques are sorely missing from the average political campaign. After the 2016 election, she wanted to empower progressive candidates with strategies that could reach a wide base of young voters. Her political awakening led her to use her skill set to help progressive candidates run better campaigns—and engage more young people in politics.

Suraj explained how the space was a starting point for their shared goal of expanding the electorate. At the most basic level, that meant the doors were always open—especially on Wednes-day evenings from five to seven p.m., when the campaign hosted town hall happy hours. Those discussions were grounded in more than 110 pages of policy proposals, including a call to de-fund ICE and one to expand labor rights of sex workers. More broadly, Suraj's mission meant not catering only to the people who were already voting, but instead growing a wider base of customers, who would be engaged at the local level well after this election.

According to Suraj's campaign statistics, the Fourteenth District saw the highest turnout ever for a June primary, increasing turnout over 270 percent since the 2016 primary, with a 797 percent increase in millennial participation from the previous election. Forty-seven percent of all voters hadn't ever participated in a primary, or were participating for the first time in more than a decade. "In the end, our eighteen thousand votes and overall primary turnout shattered New York June primary records," he told me afterward. "In fact, it was more votes than AOC or any other candidate in the state (except for my opponent, who also felt the heat of a challenge and spent a ton of money to mobilize her voters)." His goal was to invigorate the health of democracy in his district, and it worked.

That's not how campaigns are usually run. Instead, politicians raise a ton of money and then spend a lot of it on voter files. They identify the kind of people who are already probably going to vote, then hit them with robocalls and mailers. Suraj and Anjelica wanted to try to run this campaign without that antiquated strategy. To most politicians, this would seem inconceivable, if not blasphemous. For incumbents, there is little incentive to bring new voters into the fold, or make any attempt whatsoever to mix things up.

The stock campaign strategy underscores a major issue in American politics. There's the sense of inefficacy, and then there's a scope of oppression that ranges from a lack of constituent outreach to outright voter suppression. The fact is that many of our elected officials are not making it easy on purpose. If the people in power wanted us to participate in our democracy, there would be easy, rolling, online registration, and, ideally, online voting (protected by secure identity verification). Instead, sometimes even determining where and when to vote in the primary can be difficult. Incumbent politicians often make little to no effort to bring their constituents to the polls. (This problem is encapsulated in *Knock Down the House*, the Netflix documentary that follows Alexandria Ocasio-Cortez's campaign. She sits on her couch, reading a postcard from her incumbent opponent, Joe Crowley. She unpacks Crowley's lack of specific commitments, but the most telling detail of his mailer is that the date of the primary is nowhere in sight.)

At the most basic level, it is a reality that a lot of Americans aren't voting because they don't know how (or when, or where, or for whom), and that's no accident. The majority of us seem to at least be aware of the importance of voting. And yet, most local elections see less than a tenth of eligible voters showing up to the polls, and even the general elections barely elicit ballots from half the country. In the previous election, Suraj's primary opponent, Carolyn Maloney, had turned out an abysmal 8 percent of all eligible voters. The fact is that people in power have deliberately made it difficult to participate in democracy at even the most basic level of voting.

In confronting the shameful reality of low voter turnout, politicians scapegoat their constituents, and the media actively aids in the smear campaign when news coverage turns the lens on voters rather than the elected officials who have abdicated their democratic duty. We routinely see low turnout statistics blamed on voters themselves—especially in the case of young people. According to the Census Bureau, since 1971, when eighteen-year-olds were granted the right to vote with the Twenty-Sixth Amendment, the youth voter turnout rate has averaged about 40 percent in presidential elections and 20 percent in midterms. Recently, these statistics have inspired headlines like "When It Comes to Politics, Do Millennials Care About Anything?" from the *Atlantic* or "Millennials' Surprise: There Isn't an App to Solve All Problems" from the *Chicago Tribune*, which encapsulate the overarching myth of youth apathy in framing alone. After each election, there are countless articles asking why young people don't vote, blaming our lack of engagement on narcissism and/or frivolity. Most are about as rigorously supported as claims that we don't own homes, because avocado toast.

Suraj explained all of this to me in terms of his campaign, then summed up the whole mess in a single line: "Politics is the only industry that chastises its customers for not wanting to buy a shitty product."

A VORTEX OF CORRUPTION

So, how did the product get so shitty? When did politicians stop regarding the American public as their main customers? Why is this the state of our democracy today? The answer is, of course, moneyed interests, which is the most obvious way in which the political-industrial complex rears its head. (By the way, I'm picturing Wolf Blitzer's face on, like, Smaug's body as the visual here, but please use whatever works best for you.)

The nuts and bolts of that cycle of power look like this: Elections are increasingly expensive, which means politicians are largely competing for money to fund their campaigns and secure votes. It all comes down to money and votes. These two currencies come from five kinds of potential "customers": partisan primary voters, special interests, donors, average voters, and nonvoters. "Parties prioritize the customers that most advance their interest," Gehl and Porter explained in their study. Because fundraising has become so critical to securing elected office, the influence of donors and special interests far outweighs that of other constituents. In the rare moments when candidates cater directly to constituents, it is mostly to the extremely limited pool of partisan primary voters, who are more effectively targeted with voter files. That means politicians are largely unconcerned with the average voter and have no reason whatsoever to galvanize nonvoters, which pretty much means that they are ignoring the entire fucking country.

In *Requiem for the American Dream*, the philosopher and activist Noam Chomsky famously refers to corporate and political leaders as the "masters of mankind," a phrase first used by Adam Smith in *The Wealth of Nations* in 1776. Rather than the merchants and manufacturers Smith depicts, that group is now comprised of financial institutions and multinational corporations, and they are driven by the same "vile maxim": "all for ourselves, and nothing for other people."

Chomsky explains that public policy is largely dictated by

these "architects of society," and their power is only intensifying as the political-industrial complex grows. "Concentration of wealth yields concentration of power," he said. "Particularly so as the cost of elections skyrockets, which kind of forces the political parties into the pockets of major corporations. And this political power quickly translates into legislation that increases the concentration of wealth."

Such is the warped incentive structure depicted by Gehl and Porter through the lens of industry competition: American politics is trapped in a vicious cycle in which politicians endlessly vie for campaign financing. Then they get elected and, out of allegiance to those who made their position possible, create further legislation to endow the stronghold of big money, becoming more and more accountable to donors and special interests and less accountable to constituents. Money begets power, which begets more money, and the gap between public will and public policy grows ever wider. It's a self-sustaining vortex of corruption, and the whole mess is held firmly in place by, yes, you guessed it, the political-industrial complex.

Gehl and Porter focused on the political-industrial complex as the means by which the two-party system maintains its stronghold on power, creating extremely high barriers to entry for additional political parties. But beyond that, it creates extremely high barriers to entry for anyone who isn't a high-currency customer of the system (aka the majority of Americans). It is the force by which we've ended up with an oligarchy; the country is run by a ruling class that answers only to donors and the few old folks who show up to vote. The whole thing is a self-fulfilling prophecy of impotence: because of the political-industrial complex, it is incredibly hard for any individual person to have a voice in politics, and because it is incredibly hard for any individual person to have a voice in politics, most of us don't even bother.

The urge to push against this state of submission is smacked down by the political-industrial complex as if in a game of Whack-A-Mole. When I understood American citizens as customers of the political industry, I thought of sociologist Don Norman's influential work *The Design of Everyday Things*. There, Norman parsed some of the reasons certain products are hard to use. "Many of the rules followed by a machine are known only by the machine and its designers," he wrote. "When people fail to follow these bizarre secret rules, and the machine does the wrong thing, its operators are blamed for not understanding, for not following its rigid specifications." Norman used the example of doors: The purpose of doors is to be opened and closed, and the users of doors should know how to do that. Except, sometimes it's not so easy to open a door. Sometimes, you don't know whether to push or pull, and you puzzle over it, chastising yourself for being a total moron, when really the door is badly designed. In politics, the door is about as accessible as Platform 9¾. Without awareness of the "bizarre secret rules," you've got no way of entering.

With most consumer goods, crappy design is a failure that companies try to fix to satisfy their customers. In the political-industrial complex, it's a deliberate means of further consolidating power for those who already have it.

Working to maintain the political-industrial complex, gate-keepers like pundits, lobbyists, and campaign managers keep the average citizen at arm's length by coding politics' "bizarre secret rules" in a process known as professionalization. Take, for example, the idea that political campaigns must be conducted with calls to voters listed in voter files, made from some depressing-AF office space. That's supposedly "just the way things are."

The political scientist and researcher Gerry Stoker described this process in his book *Why Politics Matters*. Through professionalization, politics has come to be practiced largely by a specialized group of experts, who operate according to "norms they understand and support [that] lack any strong connection back to the citizens they allegedly serve." This creates a world of bizarre secret rules that further separate leaders from the public they are meant to serve. "The cadres of actors who run democratic politics have developed an inward-looking culture that fails to engage and inspire many ordinary citizens," he explained. "The political system is run by 'them' (the political leaders, lobbyists, spin doctors, and journalists, and their bosses) and seems to have little meaningful engagement for 'us' as citizens."

At all levels of government, we have lost sight of the function of our elected officials. It is their job to serve the public—not big donors or lobbyists. They work for us, and ought to be making decisions that reflect the will of the majority, or otherwise face losing their seat. Instead, the political-industrial complex has made it acceptable for our representatives to entirely reject input from constituents once in office. Many have totally abdicated their responsibility as representatives of democracy, and we have allowed it to happen by accepting that a lack of accountability in office is "just the way things are."

THE DEMOCRATIC BYSTANDER EFFECT

It's no mistake that, prior to the 2016 election, young people came to understand politics as a thing important men do off in a room somewhere, possibly while wearing boat shoes. The vortex of corruption is the source of the idea that there's no point in trying, because, anyway, it wouldn't make a difference. Here lies the crux of the issue: the political-industrial complex silences our voices, perpetuating its own inevitability, as its participants convince us we have no reason to even attempt to speak up.

That's where the reciprocal loop of disengagement comes in—we don't, because we think we can't. As Gehl and Porter put it, "Too many people—including many pundits, political scientists, and politicians themselves—are laboring under a misimpression that our political problems are inevitable." This fatalism stops us from taking action. Instead, we submit to a "trust the process" mentality. But when we accept the status quo, we ignore our role in the political-industrial complex and only succeed in upholding it. We are all complicit.

To be clear, it's true that the average citizen has an infinitesimal impact on politics. For example: the majority of Americans favor gun reform (66 percent, according to a February 2018 poll by Quinnipiac University Polling Institute), a more comprehensive health-care policy (60 percent say it should be the government's responsibility, according to an October 2019 report from the Pew Research Center), and improved social security (12 percent are "very satisfied," according to a Gallup survey conducted through 2018), and yet none of these issues are prioritized by the legislature. In 2014, researchers from Princeton and Northwestern developed a statistical model for measuring this disconcerting reality by looking at 1,779 policy issues and controlling for variables like elite business groups. Their finding? The average American has "near-zero" influence. In technical terms, our voices are "statistically non-significant." The relationship between the governors and the governed has become almost totally authoritarian: they set the terms of the conversation and then barely uphold the charade of pretending we have a say, and there are statistics to prove it.

It may be overwhelming to consider that the political will of the individual is approximately as impactful as making wishes at 11:11, but together we can change that. The function of democracy was never about enacting what any one of us wants; democracy is intended to reflect the will of the collective. In failing to contribute individual action, we deny ourselves the force of public will, thereby further allowing the political-industrial complex to place greater and greater influence in the hands of our corporate and political power brokers. The only reasonable way to combat this is for each of us to commit to the daily work of democracy. That is the way individual action can build to collective impact. Only then will the many have a shot against the few.

At first, this process will make us all feel like a couple of butterflies trying to scream over a state-of-the-art speaker system. The path to a truer, more equitable democracy doesn't come with shortcuts. It will be laborious and mind-numbingly incremental. It will require overhauling fiscal policy and re-formatting the voting process in a way that emphasizes electorate building, accountability, and recallability for our elected officials. Along the way, our voices will still have "near-zero" influence on their own, but collective power requires all of us to work together, and, goddamn it, we have to at least try. The post-Trump awakening marks a rare opportunity for the realization of agency to build to real change.

The revolution will require us to show up—to vote, and to practice a daily habit of democracy. The political-industrial complex depends upon our disenfranchisement. It is in each of us doing our part that we make change possible.

The political-industrial complex is the true villain in the death of democracy, but we're all accomplices. It's like we're watching the American project be killed in the way of Kitty Genovese, the apocryphal victim in the murder case that is often used to demonstrate the psychological phenomenon known as the bystander effect. You've probably heard this story before. Kitty was killed on the way home to her Kew Gardens apartment building in 1964. Inaccurate reporting held that thirty-eight of Kitty's neighbors watched her be stabbed to death across three separate attacks, allegedly failing to come to her defense or call the police. The case entered the public mind as a fable on the need for personal responsibility in the face of passive assumption. Surely, they thought, someone would do something. And so, no one did anything at all.

Kitty's tragic fate is the stuff of legend at this point—it's since been proven that most of the thirty-eight neighbors only heard muffled sounds outside—but the takeaway offers a sturdy analogy for our failing state of governance. Democracy is being stabbed to death, and there are a helluva lot more than thirty-eight witnesses. It is through "statistically non-significant" individual action that we build to the collective power required to overthrow the political-industrial complex. This is the part where we decide to save ourselves.

CHAPTER 4

POLITICAL ALIENATION

An awakening is only fully realized when it becomes impossible for things to go back to the way they were. In order to understand what is changing in our approach to politics, I knew I had to unpack the before state.

There was this ineffable weight of inaction that predated the urgency of the 2016 election. The young people I spoke to could only describe this feeling once they left it behind, and even then, they couldn't name it. "I had always been interested in politics and progressive causes, but had never been especially active," a then-twenty-three-year-old grad student named Cosette wrote to me in an email. "The last year has changed my outlook, and my behavior." For many, the change happened overnight. "It was a very sudden shift from apathy to activism," said Madison, who was nineteen at the time. "I think a part of it was feeling I needed to vote responsibly once I turned eighteen, wanting to be able to participate in discussions, and generally [feel] like I was an adult and part of society." A young man named Axel, who had recently turned eighteen, described the shift in more visceral terms. "It was like somebody had decided to throw a cold bucket of ice water on me while I was sleeping," he said.

In hopes of better understanding the way we operated before our awakening moment, I started reading sociological work on alienation, and soon found my way to the researcher who began working to make the concept accesible more than fifty years ago: former chair and longtime emeritus professor of UCLA's sociology department Melvin Seeman.

When I reached out to arrange an interview, Seeman got back to me faster than almost any interview subject I have ever emailed and said he would be happy to speak to me. He provided a disclaimer, though: "I celebrated my 100th birthday just about a month ago," he wrote. "To my knowledge the cognitive deficits are minimal . . . just thought you ought to know (if you don't already)." He also suggested that I call him "Mef." I obliged, and also texted several friends that I wished Mef were my grandfather.

On our call, I explained how my peers described their political awakenings with startling similarity. Across the country, at Louisiana State University, Colby College in Maine, Northwestern in Illinois, Penn State, and New York University and Fordham in New York, among others, I kept hearing the stories of young people who had, in the wake of the 2016 election, moved from passive interest to active involvement. I told Mef I wanted to figure out why we had felt such acute political alienation to begin with.

Mef was chuckling. I thought I had been too earnest. "I'll tell you why I'm laughing," he said. "I'm laughing because I was just talking to my son about this last night!" His son, Mef continued, visited often these days, as his wife of nearly seven decades—which is not a short time, young lady—had died four years ago. This is how much of our interview went. I wanted answers; Mef wanted to tell me about living out the twilight of his life in his Malibu beach house. (Which, to be fair, sounded positively delightful.)

Eventually, we got back to why Mef was chuckling. The night before, during their regular five thirty p.m. wine chat, Mef and his middle-aged son found themselves, once again, discussing current affairs. Both were pessimistic about the state of our democracy but were optimistic about the actions of the students of Marjory Stoneman Douglas High School who, in the wake of the school shooting in 2018, had launched an impassioned campaign for gun control. Was it possible, Mef and his son wondered, that there might be a surge in civic participation on the horizon?

A SOMETIMES THING

What they were talking about, really, was political alienation, and how young people seemed to be breaking free of it—once again. As a sociologist who wrote one of the seminal papers on the topic in 1959, Mef would know. He introduced the concept of political alienation to the discipline of sociology. (He'd be the first to tell you there are European Marxists who think he's taken Karl's understanding of the term too far out of its original context of explicitly capitalist critique, but that's a conversation for another phone call, if you don't mind.)

Mef first became interested in the concept while leading a course on ethnic prejudice and personality at Ohio State University in the 1950s, where he was pursuing his doctorate in social psychology. He didn't feel the assigned textbook provided a comprehensive definition of the term "alienation" as it applied to his field. "I thought, 'I can't teach this stuff if I don't know what I'm talking about,'" he said.

In that first research paper, he categorized alienation into five "types": powerlessness, meaninglessness, normlessness, isolation, and self-estrangement. These five types are broken down in order "to make the traditional interest in alienation more amenable to sharp empirical statement," or, for those nonacademics among us, to explain it without making you want to impale your eyeball with a highlighter.

See, political alienation is almost impossibly difficult to describe, not only for those experiencing it but for those trying to make it "more amenable to sharp empirical statement." Alienation is a lack of something. It's a void. A block. If "alienation" were the answer to a riddle in *Alice's Adventures in Wonderland*, the Mad Hatter might say, "It is less than what it is, it is what it's not." Political alienation is easier to describe in terms of its positive opposite: a moment of intellectual and emotional realization that renders inaction impossible. Or what you might call a political awakening.

It only becomes possible to talk about political alienation once you have gone through a political awakening, and that's what began happening when the term first popped up, starting in the late fifties. Around the time Mef wrote his paper, he noted the term appearing across academic research and casual conversation. Political alienation, Mef explained, is best understood as "a sometimes thing." It is discussed in some decades and not others. As re-alienation increased, the term "political alienation" dropped out of conversation. Mef estimated that by the 1980s, it had disappeared almost entirely.

"A sometimes thing?" I asked.

"By 'sometimes thing,' I mean that alienation comes and goes," Mef explained.

In the five decades since Mef had first begun researching political alienation, he had seen the term shift in and out of view. As the feeling of awakening emerged, so would the term for describing the "before" state. As Mef sees it, the circumstances for political alienation change over time, and so does the way we talk about it. A sense of powerlessness can dissuade people from participating in social movements or be recognized as a galvanizing factor—like it was for many young people in the 1960s, who went on to participate in antiwar protests and the civil rights movement.

"Look at your own example!" Mef said. "Your interest in alienation wouldn't really have happened fifteen years ago. It was a dead topic at the time. There is a historical resurgence about alienation that is very relevant here."

This resurgence of alienation dovetails with the rise of "woke." The term, introduced through the Black Lives Matter movement, has saturated social media as shorthand for understanding the true nature of inequality. Black Lives Matter forced a long overdue reckoning with the racial oppression that defines American life. The movement has fundamentally altered the political landscape by pushing systemized dehumanization to the center of the conversation. Rather than fighting any specific injustice, Black Lives Matter centers on institutionalized oppression. Through online discussions that both organized and cataloged the protest of police brutality, the idea of wokeness entered the conversation as a way of understanding tragedy in the context of systemic racism. Being "woke" is about processing atrocities through the system that allows them to routinely occur. This questioning and the movement responsible for it ignited many political awakenings long before Trump announced his campaign.

As with the Black Lives Matter movement, there are moments in history—both recent and long past—that recall aspects of what's happening now. My call with Mef wasn't the first time I saw a connection between the 1960s and our current political moment. On multiple occasions, older men—and at least three men named Mark—have messaged me to be sure I've noticed the similarities. "Something is happening, Lauren," wrote one. "The energy feels the same as it did then." In both moments, an event or series of events prompted widespread political awakenings. Strong political opinions became a social necessity. And when you are compelled to form a strong political opinion, political action tends to follow.

The event that spurred our awakening moment was Donald Trump's election. In the 1960s, it was the Vietnam War. Establishment politics led the country into an unconscionable war abroad, and the draft dragged the issue of US imperialism into American living rooms. Compelled service meant that most of the country was faced with the possibility of either going off to war or sending a loved one off to war. In January 1969, a Gallup poll found that 52 percent of Americans felt that entering Vietnam was a mistake, and 39 percent approved. Young people were most aggressively opposed to US involvement in Vietnam. That spring, a Gallup poll of students found that 69 percent identified as "doves," or proponents of peace, while 20 percent identified as "hawks," or proponents of the war. It was the most embittered divide in public sentiment since the Civil War, and there was no escaping it. By 1970, 52 percent of Americans knew someone who had died or been injured in Vietnam. The result forced the public to develop a stance on US policy. There was no such thing as being "meh" on the Vietnam War, and the same is true of Trump.

The civil rights era occurred in tandem with the antiwar movement, which peaked at the end of the sixties, but started before the decade began. Rosa Parks refused to give up her seat on a segregated bus in 1955, and it was in 1960 that African American students sat in passive resistance at the Woolworth's lunch counter. In July 1964 President Lyndon Johnson signed the Civil Rights Act. The legislation outlawed discrimination based on race. Although, any resulting progressive idealism took a swift turn a month later, when Congress signed the Gulf of Tonkin Resolution, allowing the president broad power to send US forces into Southeast Asia. This action helped the Johnson administration escalate its efforts in an unpopular war;

the Vietnam draft lottery would come five years later, on December 1, 1969.

Men between the ages of eighteen and twenty-six were forced to offer their lives for what many of them saw as an unjust war. It pushed young people to interrogate not only traditional authority figures but overarching cultural norms. They asked, as we do now: who makes the rules? The political awakening of the sixties spread from opposing the war to challenging the presiding hierarchy of modern society.

These ideas became entangled in the growing counterculture. Before he was asasinated in 1968, Martin Luther King Jr. notably condemned the war in a speech where he called the United States the biggest perpetrator of violence in the world. Between August 1969 and August 1970, there were at least nine thousand protests throughout the country, many beginning on college campuses, from antiwar demonstrations to the protests of the civil rights movement, which worked to dismantle institutionalized cruelty toward black Americans. Meanwhile, women were interrogating their place in the home and the workplace, and the laws and societal norms that kept them without the same rights as men. They fought for independence, especially through access to birth control. The LGBTQ community rallied against sex- and gender-based discrimination, beginning most prominently with the Stonewall riots in New York City in 1969. Public dissent reached a fever pitch as the sixties drew to a close. It all seemed to kick off with the protest of Richard Nixon's inauguration in January 1969, when one thousand antiwar protestors assembled in Washington, burning miniature flags and hurling rocks at the incoming president's motorcade. By September of that year, Nixon was pushed to acknowledge mainstream opposition to Vietnam. One month later, two million people around the country took part in the Moratorium protest calling for the end of the war, cementing antiwar sentiment as popular opinion.

By comparison, an estimated half million people gathered for the Women's March in Washington, DC, after Trump's inauguration in January 2017, in opposition to the president and the policies on which he campaigned. More than four million people joined the protests nationwide. CNN covered the first march with a caption asking "Women's March: Moment or Movement?" The numbers alone would indicate the latter, and that was long before the 2018 midterm elections changed the shape of Congress by electing a historic number of diverse representatives, due in no small part to the largest youth turnout in a quarter century.

There are similarities between these two historic moments, but important differences, too. During the 1960s, the political awakening included broad questioning of the presiding social hierarchy, though it didn't quite have a clear bull's-eye—at least, not in the way we have now. For example, it was possible to oppose both Nixon and Vietnam, and, to be sure, much rage was directed at the thirty-seventh president and various renderings of his rather large nose. But the war was also associated with Eisenhower and Johnson before him. Today, we have an obvious target in Trump. That has radically increased the force of the corresponding protest movement;

there is a focal point to organize around. It's crucial that the commitment to civic engagement sustains itself long after Trump leaves office, but the targeted outrage directed at his administration imbues this moment with a degree of revolutionary potential not seen since the sixties, and this time that potential is, perhaps, far greater.

Looking back at history, at moments that came close to the energy of the 1960s, further demonstrates our current opportunity to overthrow the status quo. Consider another major flashpoint in American politics: the Iraq War. Opposing the war generally meant opposing President George W. Bush. The decision to invade Iraq rested squarely on Bush's shoulders. He told the public that the US would not "allow any terrorist or tyrant to theaten civilization with weapons of mass murder" while standing in front of the Statue of Liberty on the first anniversary of the September 11 terrorist attack. Six months later, the United States invaded Iraq. Those weapons of mass destruction have yet to turn up.

Perhaps pop culture's clearest rebuke of Bush came from the Dixie Chicks. In March 2003, as Bush prepared to drop the first bombs in Iraq, the band was onstage in London. "Just so you know, we're on the good side with y'all," lead singer Natalie Maines told the crowd. "We do not want this war, this violence. And we're ashamed the president of the United States is from Texas." That sentence made the Dixie Chicks turn into pariahs so suddenly, it was as if by uttering it, Natalie had inadvertently cast a spell. Country stations began aggressively pulling the Dixie Chicks from their playlists. One station even had a "chicken toss" party, in which they threw the group's CDs and concert tickets in the trash.

The country music industry—intricately connected to Southern culture and conservatism—played a major role in the Dixie Chicks' fall from grace, but music executives and radio DJs took their cues from the overarching political climate. Even if you disagreed with the war, it was still taboo to condemn the president. That's not the case in our current political climate. Public figures have lost jobs because of early opposition to Trump, but these examples tend to be extreme. In one such instance, the comedian Kathy Griffin was fired from CNN's New Year's special after she posed for a photo shoot holding up a model of Donald Trump's severed head. She's been on multiple stand-up tours since. The Dixie Chicks, on the other hand, saw their careers go up in flames because they politely expressed shame at their own concert.

For the most part, major celebrities denouncing the legitimacy of the sitting US president now barely qualifies as news. Cultural juggernauts like Meryl Streep, Cher, Shonda Rhimes, George Clooney, Lady Gaga, J. K. Rowling, Stephen King, Robert De Niro, and Madonna have all made public rebukes of the president since his election. In September 2017, I wrote a profile of John Legend for the *Guardian* in which he called Trump "an embarrassment to the country," and I'm pretty sure the piece got more traction for his comments regarding *La La Land* (not just a white film about jazz, FYI). At this point, it is famous figures who stand in support of Trump that are outliers.

Opposing the president of the United States is acceptable in ways it has never been before. And this moment comes with another major revolutionizing factor: a paradigm shift in the way we think about people in relationship to government. The last time we saw something like it was with Occupy Wall Street.

The Occupy movement took aim at the wealth gap by focusing on the corruption of Wall Street following the 2008 financial crisis. The leaderless movement was born in July 2008 when a magazine called *Adbusters* ran a post that called for twenty thousand people to "flood into lower Manhattan, set up tents, kitchens, peaceful barricades and occupy Wall Street for a few months." The movement began in earnest with a protest that began on September 17, 2011, in New York City's Zuccotti Park.

The demonstrations also took aim at the broad scope of power held by financial institutions and multinational corporations, especially in terms of the way in which their influence creates a grossly unjust distribution of wealth. This was paramount after the recession, when the US government spent billions of dollars aiding the financial industry and car companies, while an estimated 2.6 million people lost their jobs. Many protestors called for elected officials to reconsider corporate bailouts while so many Americans struggled to put food on the table.

Occupy was leaderless by design and has been criticized for a lack of concrete demands. But nearly a decade later, it's clear that the impact of Occupy lies in the rhetoric birthed by the movement. While the protests may have lacked specificity, Occupy's participants forever altered the narrative around financial justice, or, rather, the lack thereof. Their work extended far beyond the drumbeats sounding out in downtown Manhattan. The movement soon spread to other US cities and eventually bloomed into a global movement, inspiring protests across more than eighty countries worldwide. By January 2012, less than three months after the first protest, the Pew Research Center reported that two-thirds of the country believed there was a "strong" or "very strong" conflict between rich and poor, a nineteen-percentage-point increase from the same survey three years earlier.

The rhetoric of Occupy centralized around the gap between the masters of mankind and the rest of us, framing the public at large as the 99 percent. That number is based on income statistics. By some measures, economic gains over the last several decades have led to increased wealth for just 1 percent of the population. There are other metrics for measuring wealth, but the 99 percent slogan powerfully illustrates the concept of widespread economic and political inequality, and it has been incredibly effective. In February 2012, the *New York Times* ran a piece titled "Why Obama Will Embrace the 99 Percent," codifying the term in the mainstream political conversation.

The Occupy movement brought this issue to the forefront of American political debate. Its effects reverberated long after protestors were evicted from Zuccotti Park in November 2011. Bernie Sanders's 2016 presidential campaign built on this rhetoric. The Occupy movement paved the way for the Vermont senator to run for office as a proud Democratic Socialist, a label that would have been too stigmatized to be viable in any previous general election. Instead, Sanders invoked the narrative of Occupy to become a serious contender for the Democratic nomination.

Although they didn't use the term itself, the language of the Occupy movement was, in many ways, focused on challenging the political-industrial complex. At its core, Occupy was about insisting on the collective impact of that 99 percent. It was a reaction to the economic recession but also the failures of our government—which, during the recession, turned its focus first to the financial industry and car companies. A CNN segment on the protests from September 2011 documented these connections. "I'm here myself as a free individual, to humanize the markets, and to have true, participatory democracy," one young man told a reporter. "[I'm here] to make Wall Street hear the sound of what democracy means." The camera then cut to a woman directing a group of marchers. "What kind of power?" she yelled. "People power," they chanted in response. This was the paradigm shift at the core of the rhetoric: a call for a rebalancing of power, both economic and political. Our current moment hinges on this same redemocratizing force.

I was in college for the brief and wondrous period before the original Four Loko formula was banned, and I used to describe its effects as allowing for the happiness of a wine drunk and the steadiness of a beer drunk, topped off with the wild card of a tequila drunk. Much like the recipe that supercharged Four Loko, this moment is a perfect storm of three major history-shifting factors—all of which have been documented before, though not all at once. The polarization created by the Vietnam War forced the public to question authority as the nation was compelled to form strong political opinions on which to act. Resistance to the Iraq War gave way to directly challenging the sitting president. Through its rhetoric, the Occupy movement channeled broad rage over our lack of a voice in the financial and political system. This political moment boasts these three factors: the same intense polarization, a clear oppositional focal point, and a paradigm shift in the way we think about people in relationship to power.

But I still kept coming back to the idea of political alienation. Why was it a "sometimes thing"? It can creep back in, even after a generation breaks through it. The idea of alienation was still making me feel like I wanted to down several Four Lokos, when Mef shared a story that brought the concept fully into focus.

While working as a professor at Ohio State during the Free Speech Movement, Mef wasn't only thinking about alienation in the abstract; he witnessed it firsthand. The year was probably 1967, and Mef was in his fifties (if you can believe that, young lady). He had assigned the class a project on alienation and one group asked if they could hand in something other than a paper. There had been a sudden trend of uprisings on college campuses, and they wanted to try one in the classroom. They asked Mef if they could stage a protest against his course. They asked if he would leave the room, acting as if he'd been ambushed by the disruption.

Mef thought it was a dangerous idea, but he was compelled by his own curiosity. On the condition that the class would later be briefed on the way in which this group's project was staged, he agreed to play along. The next week, the group acted as if they were disrupting the lecture, and Mef pretended to be chased out of the room. He posted up to eavesdrop outside the door. He thought the rest of his students would leave the second he left.

"The policeman was out, so I thought they would get up and go," he said, as if still amused by the whole thing years later. "But the basic fact is that they didn't! They did not. Very few people left."

Instead, almost all of his students remained in their seats, and, for the rest of the class, they discussed Mef's course design. Actually, they had quite a few grievances. There was a lengthy conversation in which they bemoaned all the things that Mef had done wrong over the course of the semester. There was overarching consensus about what they found to be lacking in the course, but also a shared feeling that they had no real input as to how it should be taught. They were just students, after all. From what Mef overheard from his post outside the door, they felt that since he was the teacher, there was nothing they could do.

The students were so brutally honest in their complaints that one young woman visited him in office hours the next day. Mef chuckled again at the thought. "She wanted to see if I was okay!" he exclaimed.

"So they were a textbook example of alienation, even in the middle of doing a project on alienation?" I asked.

"Yes," Mef said. "They talked about how they had no real input in what was happening in the classroom. They felt a powerlessness in being students. I was the professor, I was up there lecturing, and that was it. The alienation we were talking about was in the room."

It was such a perfect example, now I was the one chuckling.

Because that's what's changing now, on a grand scale. We are—as I saw after speaking to Mef—a generation overcoming political alienation. And there is power in this: the simple fact that we outnumber them.

POLITICAL SOCIALIZATION

According to a July 2017 report from the Pew Research Center, young people now comprise the nation's largest voting bloc. Millennials and Gen Z cast 69.6 million votes in the 2016 election. That was a narrow majority of the 137.5 million total votes, but our numbers are only growing. Nielsen data published in July 2017 reported that Gen Z, or those born between 1997 and 2015, now comprises 26 percent of the population. Every year, more of that demographic is eligible to vote.

That's particularly significant because of something called political socialization, or the process by which we form political beliefs. It is a dynamic process, although much of our ideology tends to be set in youth, between ages fourteen and twenty-four. Usually, beliefs formed during this period are shaped by major events on the national stage while we're growing up. What's the state of the economy? Is there a war going on? Which party is in power during most of it? Sometimes, the answers to those questions cause huge numbers of voters to shift their stance all at once, and often the shift is cemented for years to come. That's called a realigning election. Typically, realigning elections refer to voters altering their voter behavior by forming a party allegiance. Most scholars believe there was one in 1896, when the Republican Party became dominant following the economic crisis known as the Panic of 1893, and another in 1932, when the Democratic Party rose to prominence amid the Great Depression.

Looking at overall trends of political socialization in the population at large raises the question of whether a major shift is possible now given how many young people are coming of age in this moment of cultural change. What if the impact of the 2016 election had less to do with forming a party allegiance and more to do with our overall approach to democratic participation? What if Trump's presidency inspires future generations to break through political alienation to insist on political agency? What if we are on the precipice of forever rethinking what it means to be a citizen?

We are coming of age in a definitive political moment, one that could forever redemocratize America. Now we just have to do the damn thing.

CHAPTER 5

YOUTH POTENTIAL

When my article "Donald Trump Is Gaslighting America" went viral, it gave readers a label for the Trump administration's strategic use of disinformation, but, perhaps more important, it launched a conversation about young women and politics. The responses ranged from stealthy condescension to blatant patronization. Apparently, a solid number of old men in media were shocked to discover that we give a shit.

A lot of people wondered why I wanted to publish the article in *Teen Vogue*. To me, it was the outlet that made sense. Over the course of 2016, the website had been covering the election right next to pressing updates regarding Ariana Grande's ongoing style evolution. The article expanded *Teen Vogue*'s readership well beyond its typical demographic, reaching an audience who was surprised to see serious political writing directed at young women. But that was far from new at *Teen Vogue*.

During interviews in the days and weeks after my article was published, I was repeatedly asked why young people "don't care about politics."

We are told that young people don't care as if it is a matter of fact. One of the first things I stumbled upon in my research was an Advanced Placement government test prep book. "In general," it read, "youth is a time when many Americans pay relatively little attention to and have little interest in political issues. This is because most political issues have little direct impact on their day-to-day lives."

This is emblematic of pernicious misconceptions about young people. It was clear that was nonsense from personal experience alone. Certainly, I "cared" before the 2016 election. I wasn't apathetic; I was alienated. It never occurred to me that I could actually make a difference. The political-industrial complex favors the voices of the few, enforcing the fatalism that keeps the majority of the American people from participating in government. That fatalism is further compounded by the authority that is denied to young people as a fact of our youth, and young women, as a fact of our youth and our gender. The obstacles increase with each degree of marginalization separating any given person from the dominant group. Racism, homophobia, and transphobia also factor into who is taken seriously, or not. The whole thing is built to make most of us feel like we shouldn't even bother.

There is plenty of research that refutes the half-baked idea that young people just don't care. In broad strokes, the younger demographics actually tend to be more altruistic than older ones. A range of sociological research has compared millennials to more cynical Gen Xers and individualistic baby boomers and pronounced us a generation of "activist doers." Gen Z adds an equalizing mind-set to this do-gooder instinct. According to a 2019 study by the Pew Research Center, Gen Z is one of the most diverse age groups, and the youngest among us are even more likely to adopt progressive values, which they don't think of as especially progressive. (I like to think the shorthand here is that we're qualitatively less likely to be assholes, though none of the research says this exactly.)

You wouldn't know that from the way we're written about in the press. Across mainstream publications, "millennial" has come to be a word used to describe a privileged white kid younger than the writer, whom the writer finds annoying. Where millennials are most closely associated with entitlement, Gen Z is derided with the frivolity of social media, as when the *New York Times* referred to them as "the Snapchat generation." All of those dismissing young people on the basis of these stereotypes would do well to remember that, in addition to allegedly being selfie-obsessed narcissists, what we are, indisputably, is the future.

If we're talking about demographic coalitions in broad strokes, the generations that came before us created the circumstances that have defined our generation—not to mention climate change and the 2008 financial crisis. Now they want to blame us for not adequately addressing the fallout of variously shortsighted and selfish policy decisions, many of which were made before we were but a twinkle in our parents' eyes.

So where are all of the articles about how we are more likely to be passionate about social justice? It would seem that our altruism negates the stock theory of today's youth as frivolous narcissists.

The insulting ways in which young people are discussed in mainstream media became increasingly obvious to me as I continued writing for *Teen Vogue*. I started a column called "Thigh-High Politics," which extended my role as an unofficial spokesperson for young people. Once, I was invited to speak on a panel about increasing youth engagement in politics. When I got onstage, I realized I was the only person in the room under the age of thirty. It was as if the organizers thought of "young people" as some rare, exotic species, and I was the lone representative, tasked with recounting the beguiling ways of our strange breed. It would seem to me that if you are genuinely interested in getting young people involved, you might consider talking to more than one real, actual young person.

Instead, often, even in settings like that panel that purport to aim for youth inclusion, it's all derivative jokes painting us as distracted and shallow. I'm usually able to win at youth-outreach bingo by the time the speaker feigns ignorance regarding some form of social media. "I know you all love that Face App, or whatever it's called," they'll say into the microphone. (The major social media platforms are called Facebook, Twitter, and Instagram, and if you don't know that, you are revealing yourself to be a talking pile of dust, grossly out of touch with modern global communication networks. Please do better.)

It's exhausting, really. Young people are denied a seat at the table and then chastised for not showing up. Low youth voter turnout is a reality, but it is certainly not the result of apathy. The oppressive weight of the political-industrial complex alienates us from participating in politics, but, for many young people, that just means we've learned to apply our passion outside of it.

Perhaps the best way to demonstrate just how much young people care, given the do-gooder instinct, is through the juxtaposition of voting and volunteering statistics. A 2014 survey by the Harvard Institute of Politics looked at the two practices among Americans aged eighteen to twenty-nine. In midterm elections that season, millennials were just 10 million of a potential 40 million votes, but we made up an estimated 14.5 million total volunteers. As the *Washington Post* noted in their coverage of the study, that cohort "helped double the rate of volunteering in the US between 1989 and 2005 among 16–24 year olds." We're told that young people don't care, and the evidence is supposedly low voter turnout, but volunteering is a way bigger investment of time and energy than voting. Volunteering tends to be a commitment incorporated into a person's daily routine for an extended period of time. It can take less than an hour to vote, and that's including the commute to and from the polling place.

FROM PASSIVELY NAVIGATING A BROKEN SYSTEM TO ACTIVELY SEEKING TO CHANGE IT

This moment is not about suddenly caring about politics. Instead, the shift hinges on a sense of agency.

This was true of every young person I spoke to who experienced a political awakening. "My interest in politics transitioned from passive to active after the election," a then-nineteen-year-old named Sophia told me. "I was unhappy with the outcome of the election, so I decided to start modeling the change I wanted to see in the political arena." All were compelled by an urgent sense of purpose. "Before the 2016 election, I felt like I was floundering in my major, not knowing exactly what path to take after graduation," said Emily, who was twenty-one when she first emailed me. "Now, I feel focused, driven, and determined, knowing that one day, the odds are high I'll be fighting with my own name on a ticket." This was true even for people who were too young to vote. "After the 2016 election, I was heartbroken, but then a resolve came that changed the course of my life," wrote a high school student named Jahnavi. "At sixteen you can't vote, and are told there is not much you can do in government. I refused to let that be my reality and decided to get involved."

The changes in behavior varied widely. Some started more actively following the news, donating, or volunteering on campaigns. Others joined demonstrations or started regularly contacting elected officials. Some ran for office themselves. Unprecedented numbers of young people, women, and people of color were on the ballot in the 2018 midterms. Most were inspired by the things they'd said they'd always do when it was time. What changed is that they were no longer willing to wait their turn.

That's the spirit behind Run for Something, a nonprofit organization that helps progressive young people build campaigns for down-ballot elections. As Run for Something's website puts it, "Donald Trump is president, so throw everything you know about politics out the window. You're qualified to run for local office—we're here to help." Cofounders Amanda Litman and Ross Morales Rocketto initially thought theirs would be a small venture. They launched on January 20, 2017, and projected that they would help maybe two dozen candidates over the course of the year. It blew up almost instantly. Run for Something received more than a thousand applications when it launched during the week of Trump's inauguration, and they received two thousand more on National Run for Office Day, a self-created holiday, recognized one week after election day. By the end of 2017, Run for Something had helped more than fifteen thousand young people commit to campaigns across the country.

Over coffee in the winter of 2017, Amanda told me about the candidates she was working with. One of them was Heather Ward, who ran for school board and won. I was struck by Heather's story and thrilled to hear it was hardly unique. Run for Something's candidates all experienced a similar political awakening. "They cared about these things before," Amanda explained. "Trump winning is the thing that finally made them decide to run." The result of our political awakening moment is a total recalculation of what is possible.

Take the crisis of gun violence. You know the statistics. On average, a mass shooting—defined as the shooting of four or more people—occurs nine out of every ten days in this country. We are the only developed nation in which routine massacres are supposedly an unsolvable political issue. The majority of the country wants a change in policy. According to Quinnipiac University Polling Institute, as of February 2018, 66 percent of Americans favor stricter gun laws. And yet, according to the National Rifle Association, gun lobbyists, and Republican candidates—in short, the political-industrial complex—we are meant to accept the lack of solutions as an inevitability.

Each shooting is held up as a turning point—until the next time. We're at a point where only the most extreme acts of violence qualify for the twenty-four-hour news cycle. The 2012 Sandy Hook massacre that claimed the lives of twenty six- and seven-year-old schoolchildren and six adult faculty members was supposedly going to be the tragedy that led to gun reform. Four years later, the final straw was supposedly the terrorist attack at the LGBTQ nightclub Pulse in Orlando, Florida, which claimed forty-nine lives. Or the deadliest mass shooting in American history, the 2017 Las Vegas attack, which set a record with fifty-eight fatalities. With each new "last time," that *Onion* headline hobbles across our Facebook time lines once more: "'No Way to Prevent This,' Says Only Nation Where This Regularly Happens." Gun violence was seen as "just the way things are" here in America. We regarded near-constant mass slaughter with the total conviction of a shrug-guy emoji. That is, until the school shooting in Parkland, Florida.

On February 14, 2018, a gunman entered Marjory Stoneman Douglas High School armed with an AR-15 rifle and opened fire in the halls of his alma mater, killing seventeen people. In the immediate aftermath, the Parkland students launched into action, channeling their outrage to demand policy solutions. Instead of ambiguously decrying the tragedy, they got strategic. Armed with a microphone and media attention, they zeroed in on the corrupt system of money in politics, directly challenging politicians who accept donations from the National Rifle Association. Within six weeks, they organized students nationwide to protest around the country in honor of their newly formed organization, March for Our Lives. The crowd in DC alone numbered more than 200,000 people, and 1.2 million people turned out around the country. For the first time in decades of constant gun violence, something felt different.

It's not as if school shootings were new. The first "last time" was the Columbine High School massacre, a school shooting in Columbine, Colorado, where two gunmen killed twelve students and one teacher in 1999. According to the *Washington Post*, more than two hundred twenty thousand students have experienced gun violence since. And yet, in the past, in the wake of gun violence, politicians across the ideological spectrum had acted as if the best they could do was offer condolences. We're at a point where elected officials offering "thoughts and prayers" has lost all meaning. After Parkland, a meme circulated in which "thoughts and prayers" was written on a garbage truck. "Excellent news," it said. "The first truckload of your thoughts and prayers has just arrived." The takeaway is a cynical one. Behind these empty condolences lies the reality of political inaction.

But what was different about Parkland was that the victims refused to be anything but.

For most of the young people I spoke to from across the country, Trump's win was the event that encouraged them to channel their skills and passions into acts of practical citizenship. For the students of Marjory Stoneman Douglas, it was the tragedy that claimed the lives of seventeen members of their community. Their passion was there all along. See, the kids of Parkland already cared a whole lot about leaving the world a better place than they found it. The atrocity of the massacre was just the thing that made inaction impossible.

From the start, the Parkland kids refused to accept the status quo.

"We call BS," Emma González, then a senior, said in a speech that aired on CNN three days after the shooting. That clip would turn her into a leader in the gun reform movement.

"Every single person up here today, all these people should be home grieving," she told the crowd. "But instead we are up here standing together because if all our government and president can do is send thoughts and prayers, then it's time for victims to be the change that we need to see."

She continued, blaming Trump for his complicity in the gun violence crisis. "If the president wants to come up to me and tell me to my face that it was a terrible tragedy and how it should never have happened and maintain telling us how nothing is going to be done about it, I'm going to happily ask him how much money he received from the National Rifle Association," she continued. "You want to know something? It doesn't matter, because I already know. Thirty million dollars." (It's actually thirty-one.)

Emma was joined by other students, including David and Lauren Hogg, who went on to write about the Parkland massacre in a book called *#NeverAgain*.

In June of 2018, I was asked to interview David and Lauren on their work. I waited for the siblings in a locked room, tucked in the back of the top floor of the Union Square Barnes & Noble in New York City. Guards stood at intervals in the maze of bookshelves outside. I was told that David and Lauren would be escorted through a separate entrance any minute now. Bookstores don't typically have metal detectors set up outside of author Q & As, but this one came with a particular set of concerns. Earlier that afternoon, some person on social media had called David a hypocrite for traveling with armed guards. Being a gun reform advocate doesn't mean wanting all guns to disappear, but Internet trolls aren't known for doing their research.

There had been a delay in delivering the Hoggs to this event. The editors of *#NeverAgain* were alternately pacing and grimacing at their phone screens. They jumped in unison when the door swung open. A young woman wearing strappy patent-leather sandals walked across the threshold and held out her hand. "Hi, I'm Lauren," she announced. Her voice was some-how both breathy and forceful. At fifteen, she reminded me of teenage Kirsten Dunst, except brunette.

Lauren pushed a mass of wispy tendrils off her shoulder and looked back at David, along with their parents, and the two security guards who now stood at either side of the entrance. David's face was scrunched into a scowl. "Is that my Nitro?" he asked. "It is," one of the editors said, holding it out to him. He took a gulp. I reached out to introduce myself. David offered me his free hand, then took another hit of cold brew. It had been a long day, and they were only about halfway done with their scheduled media appearances.

David and Lauren arrived at Barnes & Noble after David

appeared on MSNBC with Chris Matthews. When we finished our Q & A, both of the Hoggs would head back to the network's New York studio for an appearance on *The Last Word with Lawrence O'Donnell*. The day before, after a spot on *Good Morning America*, they had appeared on *The Tonight Show Starring Jimmy Fallon*.

"I hate to talk about it," Fallon said moments after Lauren and David sat down. His voice trembled. "Lauren, what do you remember about that day?"

The fire alarm went off, they explained, and they thought it was a joke because there had already been a drill a few hours earlier. Lauren was laughing with her friends until she saw kids she knew running down the hall. She found a closet in a classroom, where she would hide for the next three hours, receiving texts like "Is that gunshots?" and "There's somebody shooting into my room. I love you guys. Tell my parents I love them." Before she escaped, Lauren got a message saying her friend Alyssa was dead. Alyssa was one of four close friends who died in the shooting.

Meanwhile, David was crouched in a dark corner of the culinary arts classroom, where he turned on his phone and started filming. He'd been working as a journalist for the local paper, and he understood the value of creating a record. David spelled this out on *Fallon*: "I started recording people, thinking, maybe if I die here, if our souls are left behind here on this classroom floor, like so many others have before us, hopefully our voices can carry on and echo through the halls of Congress to create positive and effective change for this country. God knows we need it."

"Wow," Fallon said in genuine shock. "Holy moly." His inarticulate response only made David seem braver.

David and Lauren have discussed the events of that day, and the ones that followed, before. Their memories are excruciatingly painful: David pounding the dashboard of his parents' car, shouting "Fuck" over and over, because there aren't any other words that make sense. Lauren, screaming in what her brother describes as a howl ripped from the pages of Greek tragedy. David, on the afternoon of the shooting, biking back to school against his parents' wishes, rage coursing through his veins. He explained that if he didn't do something, he thought he might burst.

That afternoon, David gave an interview outside of Marjory Stoneman Douglas. As he spoke to the camera, I could see the anger in his eyes. "We're children, you guys are the adults," David says. "You need to take some action." It wasn't long before he and the rest of the Parkland students realized they were the ones who would have to make the difference. The shooting developed their sense of political agency. But they already had the foundation of a rigorous civic education, and the passion to use it.

When the Parkland students first started making waves, there was some discussion of their privilege. Marjory Stoneman Douglas is part of a wealthy school district, meaning public school efforts were bolstered by substantial resources. However, that economic background has less to do with finances and more to do with the overall educational impact of a well-funded school district. While civic education tends to be deprioritized in public schools, the local budget meant the Parkland kids were exposed to a robust curriculum centered around leadership, speech, and debate. They were taught how money influences politics and understood how major stories played out across mainstream media.

Actually, Lauren had been preparing to debate the issue of background checks for weapons just two weeks before the shooting.

"I was kind of the debate champion, or something," she told me in that locked room at Barnes & Noble.

"Before the shooting, you mean?"

"Yes, before the shooting," Lauren said. Her mom added that she wasn't "kind of" the debate champion. "Okay," she corrected, "before the shooting, I was the debate champion."

In #NeverAgain, Lauren and David explain how that day transformed them into gun reform activists. You can see how their civic education has rendered their efforts effective. They understand the issue and point to concrete ways to fix it. The book concludes with a manifesto for the student-led gun reform movement. Their goals include funding for gun-violence research; digitalization of the Bureau of Alcohol, Tobacco, Firearms and Explosives' records; universal background checks; the banning of high-capacity magazines and assault weapons; funding for intervention programs; red-flag laws (or extreme risk protection orders, also known as "risk warrants"); federal regulation of interstate gun trafficking; safe storage; mandatory theft reporting; and, perhaps most crucially, getting as many people as possible to register and vote for gun reform legislation. This is practical citizenship in action.

The two are so articulate and steely in their resolve, it's easy to forget that in addition to being the leaders of a national movement, they are also teenagers. There was barely going to be time to eat in between their interviews, but they had all of seven minutes to figure it out in our Barnes & Noble bunker.

"Do you guys want pizza after this?" one of the editors asked.

David nodded, remaining deep in thought. "Sure, that sounds good," Lauren said, finding her twenty-ounce iced tea and sinking into a seat. I imagined her saying something similar to a friend's mom at a slumber party and not to her editor in between a series of appearances as a symbol of gun reform. I had the same thought again, moments later, when she applied lip gloss, squeezing the tube too hard. "Mom," she squealed, at once distressed and amused. "I'm having a lip gloss incident." In another life, a lip gloss incident would be the most pressing problem Lauren Hogg would be expected to solve.

Soon enough, Barnes & Noble employees knocked on the door to say it was time to start the Q & A. We were ushered through the stacks by a security team. I watched as David remained focused, as Lauren took a deep breath. They visibly steadied themselves, then walked out to cheers as they posed for the flashing cameras of the press before climbing onstage.

Few people have shouldered this much responsibility, and Lauren and David weren't even old enough to vote. During our interview, they discussed how their plan had always been to make a difference, but they thought they had to wait their turn. Lauren and David always wanted to be the change they wished to see in the world, as the archway of Marjory Stoneman Douglas instructed, but they were planning to figure all of that out after graduation.

"Before February 14, we thought we had plenty of time," Lauren and David write in *#NeverAgain*. "We wanted to do something that would make the world a better place, to fight for justice as lawyers or activists or crusading journalists, to be responsible citizens and raise good-hearted children. But first we had to finish high school." And then everything changed. For David and Lauren, the tragedy of the shooting is the thing that flipped the switch. Their political awakening was as simple as this: suddenly, inaction became impossible.

You can hear the shift explicitly in an interview David did with the culture and media website the Outline.

"You guys are kids, and there are adults who should be doing it," the interviewer begins, echoing David's quote from the immediate aftermath of the shooting. "Do you guys ever think, like, why the fuck are we the ones who are doing this?"

David barely needed to process the question before he spit out an answer. "It's like when your old-ass parents are like, 'I don't know how to send an iMessage', and you're just like, 'Give me the fucking phone,'" he says. "You take it, and you're like, 'OK, let me handle it,' and you get it done in one second.

"Sadly, that's what we have to do with our government," he continues. "Because our parents don't know how to use a fucking democracy." That comment encapsulates a stunning shift from passive engagement to active involvement brought on by a political awakening. What's really exciting is that this transformation is happening across our entire demographic. On a broad national scale, we are finally questioning authority.

A DEMOGRAPHIC SHIFT

David and Lauren Hogg's newfound political agency is exemplary, but this shift extends beyond young people with national name recognition. In fact, we can talk about it in terms of eighty million millennials.

When the Millennial Impact Report landed in my inbox, I opened it with more excitement than my first college acceptance letter. Here was a full body of research to back up what had previously been a convincing hunch. In a qualitative ethnographic study of three thousand participants intended to inform strategy for nonprofit organizations, the Millennial Impact Report concluded that the behaviors of the youngest generations in reaction to this political moment reveal a shift from passive involvement to active engagement.

I forwarded my book editor the Millennial Impact Report and wrote "PROOF" in all caps. Among the takeaways from the report was this: "Millennial engagement with causes and their interest in social issues has increased and intensified since the presidential election in November 2016." As a result? We are now "more likely to address social issues locally." We're shifting from accepting a broken system to actively seeking to change it.

There is a series of factors that set us up for this shift, according to Derrick Feldman, one of the Millennial Impact Report's lead researchers. "The do-good space has been present historically," Feldman said, "but what's really interesting about this generation is that boomers primarily had established certain infrastructure and systems, federally and in states and other spaces, to really heighten and inspire the activation of people to do good."

Part of the reason young people volunteer in such high numbers is because many of us were raised surrounded by highly incentivized opportunities for volunteering. It's part of admission to the National Honor Society and practically a requirement for applying to competitive colleges. The culture of volunteering came from a deliberate effort by previous generations. Baby boomers set up initiatives for giving back. This trend began in 1990 with Points of Light, an international nonprofit championed by the George H. W. Bush administration, which was intended to inspire volunteerism across the country.

Since Points of Light, there has been a boom in the industries that organize and support volunteerism. And this institutionalization of nonprofit organizations means that volunteering was a significant backdrop to many millennial childhoods. We were taught that giving back to the community is good, though many of us—thanks, in part, to subpar civic education—were not taught that often the most effective way to do that is by getting involved in politics, particularly at the local level. According to the Millennial Impact Report, in the wake of the 2016 election, that's changing.

The youngest generations seem to be drawing from passion for social justice to inform political action. What changed is that we are no longer willing to wait our turn.

"The foundation is there," Feldman explained. "Now these things are just kind of naturally bubbling up, because we're rehashing a host of social issues in the country right now."

This natural "bubbling up" is being accelerated by social media. Watching one person raise their voice can be contagious. "Usually, when you share something online, you're now looking for some validation from some others who believe like you, and once they do that, they kind of move beyond that space of, 'Wow, I'm not the only one, others are sort of validating,'" Feldman said. "From there, that's where the organizing begins to happen, and people start to say, 'Actually, I am one of many that believe the same thing, and it feels comforting, and now I'm going to go the extra mile.'" In other words, individual action is building collective power across the youth demographic.

Along with a notable spike in political engagement, researchers found significant dismay with the political system. In the Harvard Institute of Politics' 2018 survey of millennial political attitudes, they asked participants to rank the factors that are "responsible for existing problems in American politics and society." Measuring responses from both Democrat- and Republican-identifying millennials, Trump came fifth—after politicians, money in politics, the media, and structural racism. Seventy-seven percent of Democrat-identifying participants blamed Trump, but the same number blamed politicians in general, and that gets to the crux of this awakening moment: we are asking who makes the rules that govern life in this country, and demanding a role in the process.

These studies put all of the stereotypes into perspective. It all comes down to what our generation values—and our reputation as crafted by mainstream media doesn't tell the full story. We're not investing in home ownership—or diamonds, for that matter—in large part because of crushing student debt. We're not entitled, we're workaholics in pursuit of constant self-betterment that often turns to burnout. We're sure as hell not apathetic. Actually, we care so much it hurts sometimes. The difference now is that we have finally connected that passion to a sense of political agency.

This is our chance to build a future in which every last American citizen knows exactly how to use a democracy. Baby boomers built the infrastructure for our generation's do-gooder instinct. We, too, can set the stage for those who come next. I hope we'll cultivate a culture of political agency in which all Americans feel empowered to play an active role in the political conversation as soon as they are equipped with a fully functioning frontal cortex.

Gone are the days of waiting our turn. We've been wildly underestimated, but we're just now getting started.

CHAPTER 6

GETTING PAST THE GATEKEEPERS

What comes to mind when you hear the word "politics"? Up until the 2016 election, for me, the word might have conjured a pair of boat shoes or the guy I met in college who introduced himself to everyone by saying he was going to be president someday. There are supposedly certain interests that go with politics and other interests that don't, certain people who get to talk about politics and other people who don't. The white supremacist patriarchy overlaps with the political-industrial complex in obvious ways—oddly enough, I didn't meet any women in college who shook my hand and informed me they were headed straight to the Oval. It comes down to this: a cabal of (mostly) wealthy white men determines the parameters of the political conversation, keeping the rest of us out. In 1776 they wore wigs. Today they wear Brooks Brothers.

Before my political awakening, I had this idea that politics was off-limits, pursued only by those who qualify. It's unclear what the requirements were exactly, but it seems to be beneficial to play golf, for no apparent reason other than that wealthy white men tend to really get off on whacking tiny balls while wearing khakis.

The approved set of interests traces back to the political-industrial complex. The duopoly is supported by an interconnected set of entities, like politicians and lobbyists and corporations. The most visible among them is the media. Our elected officials enact the laws that impact our daily lives but there are also informal rules in place. Across print and broadcast news outlets, gatekeepers set the terms of the political conversation, asserting a set of bizarre secret rules that make the average person feel disinterested or, worse, unwelcome. I've read the Constitution several times, but I can't quite find the place where it says political conversation has to be painfully inaccessible and/or just plain boring. Gatekeepers seem to decide what is acceptable, respectable, and normal, what is qualifying or disqualifying, and it feels endlessly authoritative. That is, until you realize it's all fucking made-up.

THIGH-HIGH POLITICS

I saw this clearly when I agreed to an interview with Tucker Carlson on Fox News.

Carlson uses his platform to promote nationalist paranoia, a role that has made him a darling of the openly racist neo-Nazi website the Daily Stormer. According to an independent researcher interviewed by BuzzFeed, Carlson was featured in 265 articles on the Daily Stormer between November 2016 and November 2018. Another stunning example of Carlson's brand of hatred came in December of 2018, when he used his eight p.m. news hour to claim that immigration "makes our own country poorer and dirtier and more divided." The segment included a picture of literal garbage. More than two dozen companies pulled their advertising in response.

But this was before all of that. Almost exactly two years before, as a matter of fact. I remember, because it was the day before Christmas Eve, when I received an email from a Fox News producer inviting me on the show. I thought my life had gotten crazy after my article for *Teen Vogue* went viral. I was not even remotely prepared for what would happen next.

When I agreed to an interview, I just knew it was the source where my parents had first heard right-wing fan fiction like the conspiracy theory about Hillary killing Vince Foster in the woods. I did a Google search for Tucker Carlson. Whoever this talking bow tie was, I thought I could handle it.

The producer wanted to know if I would discuss the Ivanka plane mess. That all feels like approximately twelve lifetimes ago, but maybe you remember it? We've since had lengthy discussions about whether politics ought to be paramount in public settings, like when Sarah Huckabee Sanders was denied service at the Red Hen in the summer of 2018. The Ivanka plane mess was similarly centered on the matter of civility, which, by the way, is yet another gatekeeper concoction. Made-up Rule #987 holds that you must be polite to people who work in support of authoritarian regimes.

In this case, instead of Sarah at the Red Hen, it was Ivanka on JetBlue for no apparent reason. There was speculation that the incoming Trump administration had angled for the president's daughter to travel commercial in order to incite controversy, and that's precisely what happened. While the plane was boarding, another passenger told Ivanka that her father was "ruining the country." "Why is she on our flight?" he asked. "She should be riding private."

The frenzied response to this episode was striking. Ivanka was coddled by the mainstream media, as if she had been attacked by a rabid bear. Really, some private citizen said basically what anyone flying on a budget airline with Ivanka Trump would be thinking. "Ivanka Trump is poised to become the most powerful woman in the world," I tweeted the day the story made its way through the news cycle. "Don't let her off the hook because she looks like she smells good." That's what got Fox's attention.

During a preinterview, a producer kept asking me whether I supported Ivanka's harasser. I didn't take the bait even on that call ahead of the segment. I knew the Fox audience would be hostile to me in their endless quest to own the libs. I wanted to disarm that strategy with reason. My dream headline was "Rare Rational Conversation on Fox News." Suffice it to say, that is not what happened.

The plan for the segment seemed to be that I would blindly defend Ivanka's alleged harasser, sending up a lamb for Tucker to slaughter. This is the stock formula for *Tucker Carlson Tonight*. Conservatives in general, and especially Trump voters, are insecure about the way the right-wing belief system is framed as ignorant. And so, they delight in watching someone on their team dunking on the supposedly self-righteous opposition. We've seen this in American political entertainment before, although it's grown bloated in recent decades. Tucker Carlson is basically what would happen if you left William F. Buckley Jr. in the microwave for too long.

His audience was waiting to see a performance that would end in blood.

But first, I had to become TV pretty. By the time I was on Fox, I'd had some experience with TV hair and makeup. At the busiest hours, it's a lot like getting your oil changed at a racetrack, and the result is usually a nightmarish makeover. On CNN earlier that month, I'm fairly certain I had three curling irons protruding out of my head at once, although I couldn't see them, because I had my eyes on the ceiling, trying to avoid getting lash glue in my contact lenses. I emerged from that chair looking like a toddler who lost her tiara.

At Fox, though, the two women who did my hair and makeup took their time. They offered me water and told me to relax. I thought they were just being friendly, but, in retrospect, it seems as if they were preparing me for battle.

A producer walked me to the studio, where I was hooked up with a microphone and seated across from the monitor. A cameraman gave me a countdown, and Tucker appeared on-screen. Within seconds, it was clear this was less of an interview and more of an ambush. I started to panic. It was clear that I would not be having a "rare rational conversation." Instead, I would have to try to escape Fox's New York headquarters without being slimed on national television.

From the studio in Washington, DC, Tucker introduced me by saying Ivanka was harassed on the plane "by a member of the tolerant left," and that I was a journalist who found it justified. I had said no such thing, but facts are of tertiary importance in the Fox newsroom. My fight-or-flight response kicked in, but before the rush of adrenaline could be directed in either direction, my own face appeared next to Tucker's in a split screen.

"Screaming at a mom and her kids on an airplane seems like a violation of privacy, and decency, and good manners," Tucker began. "And it raises the question, what are the venues where you shouldn't scream your political views at people? Would a funeral be out of bounds? Church? Her son's bris?"

I wanted to talk about Ivanka's calculated role in Trump's election, as well as her accountability once he was in office—a series of events effectively making her one of the most powerful women in the world. I giggled at "bris," searching for the best way to defuse Tucker's civility bomb. I think it is entirely ethical, and, in many cases, necessarily democratic, to express public unrest toward any of our political gatekeepers, but that seemed a bit complex for Fox News, and I saw how Tucker would twist it. He was trying to get me to say I condoned harassment. "I think what is a nonpartisan issue is that air travel is horrific," I said. Really, you should've seen his face. Saying that he looked like he'd smelled a fart is putting it eloquently.

"She's not just a mother," I continued. "She's a powerful, powerful woman, who is connected very closely to the president-elect, not just as his daughter, but in many ways, as a business confidante, as an adviser."

He cut me off, accusing me of defending Ivanka's harasser a second time, then brought up another of my tweets: "Ivanka

HAS IT ALL, and by that I mean, a job, a family, & sinister complicity in aiding the most aggressively anti-woman candidate of our time," I had written.

"'Sinister complicity'?" Tucker exclaimed. "She's his *daughter*."

He was ignoring her proximity to power, playing up familial ties with a patriarchal undercurrent that underscored her influence. Ivanka had a calculated role in Trump's campaign and, at the time, was on track to securing her own office at the White House. Framing her as merely the president's daughter was an insult to viewers' intelligence. I had to keep it together. I thought of Ivanka's robotic calm.

"She was a surrogate," I said. "Frequently throughout, she represented him in terms of women's issues. She had repeated interviews—"

"Isn't she pretty liberal, though?" Tucker interrupted. He was no longer operating under the guise of decorum in a segment that was supposedly about preserving civility.

I forged ahead, focusing on his initial question. "She did speeches on his behalf, where she represented a platform of women's empowerment," I said.

"The fact [is] she was able to balance him out on these issues, where he had defunding Planned Parenthood, and being against abortion," I continued. "These [are] typically liberal women's issues that she sort of is a cushion for. I think we need to investigate those things a little more critically, a little more rigorously, and not be blinded by the fact that she looks like she smells like vanilla."

"'She looks like she smells like vanilla?'" Tucker responded. "Who's objectifying women here?"

This went on for seven more minutes. I stayed calm. I refused to be hurled into hysteria at Tucker's prodding—and he couldn't handle my resolve. By the end, he spiraled into rage cooked out of frustration. He introduced my article for *Teen Vogue* on gaslighting, then asked, voice dripping with theatrical smugness, "Does Trump make you feel like you're crazy?"

"Oh my God." I laughed. "Are you calling me crazy? That's adorable."

"He's committing psychological abuse on you!" Tucker exclaimed. "You believe that?"

"On the American people," I said. "I believe the American people, Trump supporters, Hillary supporters, Jill Stein and her cousin, are victims of Trump's gaslighting. What I mean by that is that he frequently contradicts objective evidence, not that he is abusing me personally, and I think you're smart enough to know that, aren't you, Tucker?"

"I don't know," he said. "I just take your words at face value."

"So did you read the entire article?"

"I did," he said. "I also read 'Liam Payne is 100% Certain One Direction Will Continue,' 'Ariana Grande Rocked the Most Epic Thigh-High Boots at Jingle Ball' . . ." He kept going, pelting me with headlines from my fashion and entertainment posts for *Teen Vogue*. I tried to respond, but he only grew louder. Finally, I stopped waiting for my turn to speak.

"A woman can love Ariana Grande and her thigh-high boots, and still discuss politics."

"I know, I read *Teen Vogue*, as of today," he said.

"Those things are not mutually exclusive," I continued. "You know, now that you bring up *Teen Vogue*, we treat young women like they don't have a right to a political conversation."

Tucker laughed, called it all "dumb propaganda," then cut off the segment, but not before a parting shot at what he saw as my improper use of the word "sovereignty" in the "Gaslighting" article: "Stick to the thigh-high boots," he said. "You're better at that."

I gasped. As the split screen featuring my face zoomed out of view, I squeezed in, "You're a sexist pig." Most airings of the interview didn't catch that full audio, but I know Tucker heard it. (At the top of the next segment, he looked like he'd swallowed a bug.)

It was shocking in the moment. Here was the stealthy condescension I had been seeing since I had decided to write about politics, over and over, translated into flashing lights. Tucker was attempting to dismiss my right to the political conversation based on other nonserious interests. That's gatekeeping on display.

I could write a whole other book about how the realms of fashion and entertainment are political, but that's almost beside the point. Young women like a bunch of dumb shit, and so does everyone else. Why is it that nail art is supposedly a less respectable hobby than golf? Nail art is objectively harder than golf.

These made-up rules about what counts as "acceptable" in the political conversation are deliberately antidemocratic in that the majority is disqualified from participation. Politics is not reserved only for those who fill the mysterious requirements for qualification. The political conversation is for everyone, and it should go without saying that everyone should be able to have serious and nonserious interests. Politics isn't separate from our lives; it defines it. Or, put another way, we have to be able to enjoy our lives while interrogating the question of how we ought to live together.

Tucker Carlson's philosophy of political respectability reflects a grander ethical failing of our media gatekeepers. Tucker would be more accurately described as a bully than a journalist, but we see quieter versions of this behavior across political news. The presentation of political news is often tedious enough to induce a headache, and that totally misses the purpose of journalism. The role of the journalist is to empower the public with information required to participate as citizens. Part of that work involves making politics accessible and even entertaining. It is our job to make the significant interesting.

As the youngest generations rewrite the political order, it is crucial to use the things that bring us joy to bring us power. That can mean interests that are seen as gendered, like loving shoes or pop stars, but it extends beyond the obvious sexism cooked into the phrase "Stick to the thigh-high boots" to really anything that is even remotely fun.

An excellent example of this is the rise of the Harry Potter political meme. As young people became more politically aware in the wake of the 2016 election, the wizarding world was often mined for analogies to better understand our rapidly unfurling democratic crisis.

Dumbledore's Army was frequently invoked in demonstrations. I saw at least a dozen Women's March signs saying that Hermione would not stand for this. Various members of the White House cabinet have been likened to Death Eaters (Betsy DeVos as Dolores Umbridge is honestly inspired), and, of course, Trump himself has been compared to Voldemort. It makes sense. Millennials are, in no small way, defined by J. K. Rowling's universe, and Generation Z has developed a similar affection for Hogwarts. The content of Harry's epic saga also makes for an apt paradigm for processing our political moment. The books valorize courage and good character, especially when it comes to standing up to bureaucrats and dictators using fear and hate to cling to power.

The same sort of person who would say "Stick to the thigh-high boots" might frame Harry Potter memes as juvenile, but it can be an incredibly effective way for young people to make sense of politics. As it turns out there is a nonprofit dedicated to exactly that effort. They call themselves the Harry Potter Alliance.

ACTIVISTS WITHOUT THE ACTIVISM

I had been thinking a lot about the energy of fandom in general when I discovered HPA during VidCon in June 2017 after a lanky fifteen-year-old boy asked if he could take a picture with me. I was surprised by the request but figured he might have heard me speak about journalism and politics earlier that morning, so I smiled for his iPhone. "Thank you so much," he said, already cropping the photo and flipping through filters. "By the way, what's your name?"

It was my first time at VidCon, and the behavior of the You-Tube fans buzzing through Anaheim, California, that weekend was fascinating. The whole thing sounds a lot like an amusement park: there are bursts of synchronized howling, ringing out as if on a loop, only, instead of being incited by a roller coaster, the cries of the teens are inspired by the sight of a YouTuber who has slipped from backstage passageways into the main hall of the conference center (as if they have not been briefed on the security rules that explicitly forbid them from doing that).

I had been invited to the conference for two panels on political journalism in the context of digital media. I was approximately as exciting to most of the attendees as their history teacher, but all contributors wore the same bright yellow badge, regardless of the total volume of teen screams associated with their security breaches. Apparently, this was why the lanky boy wanted a selfie, despite not having the slightest clue who I was.

"All right," another yellow badge cut in, gently ushering me away from the fan. "We've gotta head to our next panel. Enjoy the con."

"Hey," he said to me, lowering his voice to introduce himself. "I'm Alex. Figured you'd wanna get away from that."

Alex was reporting on VidCon for GLAAD, and we walked to meet up with his friend Jackson Bird, who was HPA's communications director at the time. Neither of us actually had anywhere to be for the next hour, so we grabbed coffee with Jack, as I tried to make sense of what had just happened.

The conference had seemed unfamiliar before, but now I felt like I was on another planet. Jackson, with years of attendance under his belt, was used to this kind of thing. I listened intently as he broke down the frenzied thinking behind the photo op.

Much of the fandom associated with VidCon was attached to a more general excitement over the potential for influence, and so my status as a creator was enough to warrant a selfie, even without any information about what I was creating.

There was an abundance of directionless energy in need of a focal point. I wondered: what if there was a way to apply that passion to civic engagement? I had recently spoken to one of Hillary Clinton's 2016 election coordinators, who recounted the crazy-eyed reaction from teenage recruits: they would shake and cry, freaking out to the point of hyperventilation. He'd seen this overwhelming intensity even on nonpresidential campaigns in the past, likening it to Beatlemania. I told Jack about this and bemoaned the lost potential in fan energy. If only it could be translated into political action.

"I know what you mean," he said. "A lot of fans are activists without the activism." That's when I learned about the Harry Potter Alliance.

Jackson had years of experience working for HPA, which uses the hero's journey as a way to explain what makes for effective political action. The group hosts various events and meetups throughout the year, but with four full days of translating fandom into activism, the Granger Leadership Academy is easily the most ambitious, and that's what led me to Tucson, Arizona, in March of 2018.

GLA uses the cultural currency of the Harry Potter universe as an easy access point. That model inspires every aspect of the event, including its vibrant website description. "Years ago," it reads, "a woman by the name of Hermione Granger—you may have heard of her—was reflecting on her own heroic journey, and everything she'd learned along the way about being an activist. She made plenty of mistakes, and was lucky to have a group like Dumbledore's Army (and access to a well-stocked library) to help her grow—but what about all of the emerging heroes out there who didn't?

"She reached out to the many friends she'd made over the course of her career—superheroes, rebel alien gems, bending masters—and together they founded the Granger Leadership Academy, a place for the world's next heroes to get the training they need," it continues. "Now the Academy appears each year for a weekend of intensive training, but Academy Alumni work every day to resist forces of hate and transform the world for the better. Together, they're writing a story where the heroes win. Will you join them?" That March, two hundred trainees, who had read that description and perhaps said "Hell yes" out loud, would assemble in a Tucson Sheraton. I decided to join them.

After two flights, a layover, and an entire carton of coconut water spilled in my purse, I arrived in Tucson mumbling about how this experience had better be goddamn magical. I shuffled into the first keynote of the conference, not intending to fully open my eyes until after lunch. But when I walked into the room, what I saw gave me more energy than I could ever hope to procure from a cup of burnt hotel coffee.

"Good morning!" said one girl in a voice so warm and welcoming that it took me a second to realize I had never met her before. By then, she was gone, on the way to her table, greeting every attendee she passed with the same gusto. She was wearing

Ravenclaw knee socks and a skater dress patterned with all the stars in the night sky.

The room was filled with an intergenerational crowd of two hundred trainees, though mostly young women and gender-nonconforming folks in high school and college, and two gray-haired men wearing cargo shorts, who were obviously dads. Everyone was dressed up in some capacity. There was a ten-year-old bopping around in a witch's hat, but these were not costumes so much as outfits designed for maximum self-expression. These were the kids who sat at a very specific table in high school. They were not ashamed of being unique, though they were perhaps annoyed that everyone around them had such trouble accepting their differences.

I found my place among the staff and scrolled through the *New York Times* website as I waited for the day to get started. We were in the midst of yet another soul-crushing news cycle, and I wondered how the weekend would feel in the context of this, our most recent worst week ever. Trump had thrown the stock market into distress as he proclaimed trade wars "good, and easy to win." At the same time, there was increasing evidence that Jared Kushner and Ivanka Trump had abused their White House credentials, and the *Washington Post* revealed that the president's affair with Stormy Daniels included a hush fee of $130,000, paid by his personal lawyer at the time, Michael Cohen. It was unbearable chaos, as per usual.

The earnestness pulsing through that Tucson Sheraton was enough to get me to resist the temptation to sink into the numbness of everything-is-terrible nihilism. This colorful sea of young people was about to learn how to channel their enthusiasm into effective political action, and they were thrilled about it. When the clock struck ten, Janae Phillips, HPA's director of leadership and education, who organized most of the weekend, called the room to order. As she told the story of GLA's fictional founding, I flipped through the schedule. There were breakout sessions like "Your Shiny Gender and You," in which Jack would lead a discussion group on how gender concepts apply to the activist journey; "Intersectionality: A Newt-Level Dive into the Scholarship Behind the Buzzword," breaking down the term and its history; and "The Personal Is Political," about facilitating political discussions with family, friends, and coworkers.

I tried to slip into as many sessions as possible and later that morning found "More Strong Female Characters: A Discussion of Femininity in Fandom" on the verge of getting started. The workshop leaders, Xandra and Grace, opened the session with an icebreaker. "Let's go around the room and say the first three things that come to mind when you hear the word 'feminine,'" Xandra instructed.

The room, and conference, contained few male-identifying individuals, and the vibe quickly crescendoed into something resembling a support group. "Thoughtful" came up a lot. So did "protective" and "caring," but there were also a lot of painful words, like "restricted" and "impossible." A lot of the girls in the room could only muster one adjective, then apologized for not having more. A young black woman wearing a hijab simply shook her head. I thought of all the ways these young people are kept out of conversations, even ones like these.

This workshop was about the constraints of femininity in celebrating Harry Potter, which lent a certain rawness to the discussion as it turned to a sensitive subject for the fandom: the casting of Johnny Depp in *Fantastic Beasts and Where to Find Them* after his alleged abuse of his ex-wife Amber Heard.

"I want to talk about *Fantastic Beasts*," Grace said after we had all defined "femininity." "How do we feel about the casting and J. K. Rowling's response?"

The lingering hurt from the icebreaker intensified into fury. Five hands shot up in the air.

"Yes, I feel absolutely betrayed," said a girl clutching a Hufflepuff water bottle. There was a rumble of agreement.

The Johnny Depp situation is extremely complicated for feminist Potterheads. J. K. Rowling is a survivor of domestic abuse. For her to condone an alleged abuser's role in her film was especially egregious to these fans, who had come to respect her not only for her fiction but for her values.

"The worst part is that this is a *magic world*," said a girl in the back of the room, almost surprising herself. She didn't raise her hand, but everyone was too amused to care. "There are plenty of ways to replace him last-minute."

"Also, what about movie magic?" a brunette up front chimed in. "They replaced Kevin Spacey in thirty days," she said, referencing the effort to erase the disgraced actor from *All the Money in the World* after his own abuse scandal. (Actually, it was a little over a week.)

The obvious response would be to boycott the movie, but that posed a particular problem for these superfans. See,

Fantastic Beasts is a new addition to the Harry Potter universe that was not first created in the pages of the book. The consensus seemed to be that there wasn't justification for seeing the film in theaters.

"I just can't give my money to an abuser," a Ravenclaw concluded. "But that doesn't make this easy."

The nuanced discourse in "Femininity in Fandom" was no surprise given that most of the attendees had graduated from a 101 course in social justice theory during GLA the year before. I visited the entry-level course the next morning and was impressed by its accessibility.

"There's a lot of fear around not knowing what to say," Janae said, introducing the session for a crowded ballroom. "We need to understand how our perspectives are shaped by the identities we carry and the experiences that we've had." There would be breakout group discussions later. "I want us to challenge each other's ideas and beliefs, but with empathy," Janae instructed. "Trust intent, but name impact," she continued. "Lean into discomfort. When you come out of it, you are going to be a better activist."

From there, we were presented with a PowerPoint that was mostly a glossary. *Power: access to resources and influence. Privilege: unearned access to power. Oppression: systematic use of power over particular social groups.* Janae read the definitions aloud, then noted as an aside that it was possible to be both advantaged and targeted in the context of privilege.

"All of your identities work together all the time," she said, clicking to the next slide, which defined intersectionality. "You don't necessarily need to feel guilty about privilege," Janae continued. "But think about how to undo that privilege, and why we have it." There were a lot of white people in that room, and there was a lot of nodding.

As someone who didn't fully have access to the word "feminism" until junior year of college, I imagined it would have been incredible to be fourteen, fifteen, or sixteen years old armed with the language to articulate my passion for social justice. The confidence that comes from understanding these concepts dissolves political alienation and promotes political agency. GLA made it remarkably easy. Comprehension of these terms empowered the young audience to participate in the political conversation, without the slightest regard for our gatekeepers' bizarre secret rules.

After the session ended, HPA's campaigns director, Katie Bowers, walked over to the table where I was taking notes. "So, what'd you think?" she asked.

I told her I was struck by how accessible social justice theory is when you break it down to its most basic parts. Imagine if everyone had a clear understanding of the definitions of "power," "privilege," and "oppression." It's frustrating that this isn't what's taught in public high schools as part of basic civic education.

Katie agreed. "It's all pretty easy to understand," she said, "but you have to be looking for it."

THE HERO'S JOURNEY TO POLITICAL AGENCY

This was all top of mind as I prepared to deliver the keynote speech on the second night of GLA. I figured it only made sense to talk about it through the lens of the hero's journey. I was a low-key Harry Potter fan growing up, but my heart belonged to Bilbo Baggins. My dad would read me *The Hobbit* before bed, probably before J. R. R. Tolkien was entirely age-appropriate. I visited it again in middle school and now make a habit of reading the book every few years. What strikes me about Bilbo's journey is its accidental nature. He's the hero the whole time, only it takes him a few chapters to figure that out.

Throughout *The Hobbit*, Bilbo's character development hinges on the interaction of self-determination and luck. He repeatedly emerges to rescue his crew from the brink of destruction but remains unable to take credit for his courage. Instead, he chalks it up to chance. Hobbits are usually more concerned with second breakfast than saving the day, after all.

One of the most pivotal moments in Bilbo's journey comes midway through the book. Weary of their travels, Bilbo and the gaggle of dwarves decide to rest. At this point in the trek there and back again, Bilbo surrenders to the unquestioned authority of his crew, assuming they will take care of everything. It is of crucial importance that he has recently acquired an elvish dagger, which he believes to have special powers and eventually names Sting.

Bilbo awakens to find that he and the dwarves are trapped in a heavy, sticky substance that turns out to be giant spiderwebs. It's not long before he realizes that where there are giant spiderwebs, there are also giant spiders. Propelled by the placebo effect of Sting's supposed magic, Bilbo wriggles out of the trap and frees the dwarves while dodging the eight-legged beasts who have ensnared them. He finds his courage from his belief in Sting's strength, but it's only the thing that convinces him he has the ability to fight back. His true power came from within.

Sting is a tool—just like the tools the GLA attendees acquired over the weekend. At that keynote, I said that we're all would-be heroes, reminding the audience that being empowered means empowering yourself with an elvish dagger, or the definition of "oppression," or whatever it is you might need to kill the beast. (The beast, here in our analogy, is—you guessed it—the political-industrial complex and its gatekeepers.)

The rules that govern our political conversation will be upheld until we call them out for what they are, which is to say, total bullshit. Reject the supposed qualifications for who sets the course of the political conversation by knowing with total certainty that the only requirement for acting on your political opinions is that you be informed. You have what it takes. If not? Go out and get the tools you need. It turns out we've been the heroes of this story all along.

CHAPTER 7

HOW TO HAVE A CONVERSATION

Three months after I gained national attention for defending my right to participate in the political conversation on Fox News, my parents asked me—yet again—to please not talk about politics.

The request came before a family vacation that I probably should have known was a bad idea. By March 2017, things were already worse than I had expected on election night. One week after the inauguration, Trump transcribed white nationalist ideology into public policy when he issued an executive order barring travel from seven predominantly Muslim countries. Meanwhile, the investigation into Russian election interference continued to unfurl, and the incoming administration responded with a steady stream of disinformation and distraction, including the baseless claim that President Obama had wiretapped the Trump campaign.

I'd been avoiding my parents. I was at a loss for how to face them knowing they had voted for this man, whose time in office was already defined by cruelty to marginalized communities and affection for authoritarianism. I was at a loss for how to reconcile this with my desire to believe my mother and father are good people. I thought a family vacation might help me figure out how to forgive them.

Instead, here's what happened: In between turns at Uno, my brother read aloud a tweet about then–FBI director James Comey testifying before Congress. Some combination of his being younger and a boy means the kid can get away with just about anything. I scanned my parents' faces for reactions. They didn't even look up from their cards. I had already read the story, and I saw an opportunity. "To be clear, Comey has now said Trump lied about Obama wiretapping him, so, like, that's on record," I said. "Okay, no more talking about politics! Your turn, Mom."

I immediately knew I'd made a huge mistake. My dad is heavyset and hairy, which lends a literal undercurrent to the phrase "poking the bear." He flew out of his chair.

"Do not start with that liberal bias!" he shouted.

"Liberal bias?" I asked. "That report came from the Associated Press. That is just hard news about what happened during Comey's testimony—"

That only made him angrier. He banged his fist on the glass table so hard, I thought it might shatter. The rest is a blur: cursing, door-slamming, and the emotional fallout of an upper-middle-class suburban family exploding in a flurry of Uno cards.

We spent the rest of the week in strained silence. My flippant tone is part of what instigated my dad, but I remained distressed over how angry he had become. It was like he couldn't even see me. On election night, he had tried to comfort me as his daughter. But now, the person who sat across from him was the enemy.

Rational discourse failed me. Explaining that the Associated Press is a not-for-profit newswire only enraged my dad even further. Our conversation had lost all foundation of fact. Talking about politics had once been taboo in our household, but now it was impossible. I found this absurd: writing about politics was my job. I couldn't imagine how we could have a relationship where I wasn't allowed to discuss work or what was happening in the world around us. Citing this and several other reasons, I cut off most contact with my parents after we returned from our trip. I was heartbroken. But I wasn't willing to accept that politics was off-limits, and so I decided I was instead.

Through the spring and fall, my parents and I texted a few times. They disagreed with my work but occasionally reached out to congratulate me on my accomplishments. It was strange. I felt more equipped to face off with Tucker Carlson on national television than to get through a phone call with my dad.

My parents and I saw ourselves as members of opposing teams, and we were not unique in this. Across the country, the partisan divide intensified. According to a Pew Research Center poll published in June 2016, 70 percent of "highly engaged" Democrats and 62 percent of Republicans said they are afraid of the other party.

The political-industrial complex frames stalemate competition between two parties as an acceptable political outcome. It's not. We need to talk to one another. We need debate. We need the political conversation so we can build to consensus. Instead, we have head-to-head combat—both in the media and at home—and it does not lead to anything that resembles solutions. Despite the fact that the majority of Americans support gun reform, we are meant to stomach the lack of corresponding policy as a fact of the duopoly's eternal standoff. Instead, this in-group/out-group tribalism leads to a radioactive combination of anger, frustration, and fear. The Pew Research Center should really start releasing a yearly estimate of the total percentage of ruined Thanksgivings.

The purpose of the political conversation is to work toward the goal of achieving the best possible future together. I've said you might call me "biased toward achieving equality." I think it would be more precise to say I am biased toward democracy, but, to be clear, here's exactly where I'm coming from: the American project is about building the truest, most equitable democracy. Our goal as a democratic society ought to be creating a future in which citizens share equal weight in the political conversation that governs our lives. It's not about recruiting only those who are on your side but involving as many people as possible to answer the question of how we ought to live together. The more people who vote, the better. The more we can build consensus from debate, the more we can be active in the system in a way that makes our representatives feel compelled to represent us, the closer we get to actually having government by and for the people.

Part of the reason we've gotten ourselves into this mess is

because we've forgotten how to have a conversation. We can't expect to be in dialogue with our public servants if we are not even in dialogue with one another. The discussion of political issues, especially local ones, needs to be a part of our daily lives. We have to be talking about politics to the people around us, right along with discussions regarding Beyoncé, *Rick and Morty*, or the weather.

Though the political-industrial complex renders our voices "statistically non-significant" if we don't raise them, we ratify our voicelessness. In talking to one another, we invigorate the health of the political conversation within our social circles. The effect can seem infinitesimal, but it is necessary. Through conversation, we form the political opinions that inform the actions of practical citizenship. Through conversation, we do the daily work of democracy.

Talking about politics to friends and family can be the stuff of revolution, and there are measurable effects. Perhaps the best way to look at how political conversation can build to collective power is through the concrete work of electorate building. In terms of campaigns, that means candidates should be bringing new constituents to the polls and then, ideally, continuing the work of expanding that group once in office. By discussing politics, potential voters process their identity as active political subjects who deserve a role in the process of being represented. Instead of accepting the whims of elected officials as "just the way things are," constituents insist on their role in choosing who is given political power in our government system.

ELECTORATE-BUILDING

That may seem a bit abstract. In practical terms: political movements start with people talking to one another about key issues. Certainly, no "impossible" election prospect has won at the polls without starting hundreds of thousands of political conversations. Alexandria Ocasio-Cortez proved this when she ran for Congress in New York's Fourteenth District at just twenty-eight years old. Facing off against the incumbent Democrat, Joe Crowley, who had been in office for very nearly as long as Alexandria had been alive, she beat out his hundreds of thousands of dollars in big-money campaign financing with small donations, raised through grassroots efforts. Her stunning primary victory on June 26, 2018, was due to communities' committing to her candidacy, even when winning seemed practically impossible. This was true to the extent that the *New York Times* failed to cover the campaign. When she won, it seemed as if Alexandria had transformed into a political hotshot overnight. Really, her win was the result of months and months of political conversations: people from NY-14 talking to citizens, who decided they believed enough in her vision of the best possible future to show up to the polls. Many of them had never voted before.

I saw Alexandria speak at the Socialist Alternative in Astoria, Queens, in June 2018. It was little more than two weeks before she would win the primary and exactly twenty days before she announced her lipstick color on Twitter, which would cause the tube to sell out almost immediately (Stila Stay All Day in Beso).

She wasn't a national political rock star yet, just a young woman with a dream.

That day, Alexandria was wearing no lipstick at all, in case you were wondering. I got up to shake her hand and told her we should talk more after she won the primary. She met my gaze, smiled like she already knew the outcome, and said, "That sounds good."

The crowd fidgeted with the two pieces of literature they'd been given while waiting for the panel to start. There was a small purple flyer in which Alexandria posed against a brick background. Above, the headline read: "Fighting the Queens Democratic Machine: The Alexandria Ocasio-Cortez Campaign & the Political Revolution." They also held a yellow one-sheeter outlining her campaign platform, explaining how she would fight for Medicare for all, a universal jobs guarantee, and fully funded public schools. It all seemed too good to be true. That is, until Alexandria started talking.

"Thank you all so much for having me," she said, pausing to log some eye contact. "I'm excited to be here, because it's always the first small groups of people that create movements."

Holding a microphone she didn't need, Alexandria told the story of her campaign. It started when she was working as a bartender at Flats Fix off of Union Square. In 2016, she worked for Bernie Sanders's campaign, and the election results propelled her to become more politically engaged. Alexandria explained this to the crowd without mentioning Trump. "In the past we felt, up to a time, that the world was getting better." Suddenly, it became clear this was not the case.

Alexandria started her campaign out of a grocery bag. In the early days, that's where she kept her campaign signs, rolled up behind the bar while she mixed margaritas. Momentum built gradually, and then almost all at once, but never by accident. Along with a team of volunteers, she knocked on more than 120,000 doors, moving through the streets of Queens and the Bronx until there were holes in the soles of her shoes. She accepted donations to keep going. Alexandria recalled when her campaign hit the $200,000 mark, and then announced that they had now surpassed $300,000. She described the graph of the trend as the shape of a hockey stick, miming the visuals: the numbers had coasted along, then, bam, exceeded her goal and wildest expectations, like the toe shooting off of the shaft.

Hearing those numbers, the audience sat up a little straighter, though the most impressive one was yet to come: Alexandria raised all of her money off an average donation of $22. There were nearly as many empty chairs as filled seats, but the people who were there were listening. This campaign came together as individual action built to collective power. The momentum was visible in that room. Moments earlier, that crowd would have made a church potluck seem like a rager, but now they were hanging on Alexandria's every word, wondering if her win might really be possible in their district. It was.

When Alexandria won the primary, her platform drew mainstream attention, launching discussions about her age, and race, and gender, but the most exciting aspect of her win seemed to be how she expanded the electorate. That totally changed what seemed possible in NY-14. Her victory launched a national conversation about whether such a strategy could work in the heartland, and she used her platform to insist it would. At the progressive political conference Netroots in New Orleans, she put her advocacy into essential terms: "The swing voter is not red to blue," she told a packed house. "The swing voter is nonvoter to voter. That's our swing voter."

If Alexandria hadn't hustled her way from a Trader Joe's bag behind a bar to a nationally covered congressional win, NY-14 would be filled with people who had no idea when to vote in the primary if they even knew or cared that Joe Crowley was their representative. What is most amazing about her campaign is that it galvanized an entire community with the (allegedly sensational) idea that they might be excited about the person running for office. Think about it: an elected official who might actually represent the interests of their constituents.

I'd seen this kind of thing before, the way a campaign can wake up a community. You probably haven't heard of then-twenty-six-year-old Shavonnia Corbin-Johnson, because, unlike Alexandria, she lost her campaign to represent the Tenth Congressional District of Pennsylvania, although she succeeded in expanding the electorate in similar fashion.

Shavonnia had worked in the Obama White House and always considered running for office someday. "I thought I had to be forty-five with two kids and a dog," she told me on the phone in January 2018. After the 2016 election, like so many young people around the country, she decided to stop waiting her turn. She rejected multiple six-figure job offers in Silicon Valley and started her campaign to represent the neighborhood where she had grown up in Congress. She ran on a progressive platform, not unlike that of Ocasio-Cortez, emphasizing community-based change, universal health care, criminal justice reform, and, above all else, support for working people. The model for her campaign was grounded in the idea that full-time labor should be sufficient for financial survival.

In February 2018, I drove to Pennsylvania for Shavonnia's first official campaign event. I met with Shavonnia and her team at the I-ron-ic café before the event, though "café" isn't an entirely accurate description of the place. I-ron-ic is also a gallery, thrift store, and community space, with enough characters to stock a backup Stars Hollow.

I was greeted by Dave, its proprietor, who spoke of Shavonnia as if she were his adopted daughter. He detailed her daily work habits in "the unofficial campaign headquarters." I ordered a large cup of coffee and a banana. He rang me up for $3.75 and told me refills were free. I briefly considered never returning to New York.

It wasn't long before Shavonnia's assistant, Maddie, arrived. Maddie instantly launched into the story of how she joined the campaign. It had only been a few weeks by then, and she still sort of couldn't totally believe what happened. Shavonnia had hired Maddie when she overheard that Maddie had gotten laid off at a local power plant. It had been in this coffee shop, actually. Shavonnia needed an assistant, so Dave played matchmaker. Maddie was excited, save for the fact that she didn't know much of anything about politics. "Um, you know I have no political experience, right?" she asked her new boss. "I can teach you,"

Shavonnia told her. Maddie was convinced, and once Shavonnia arrived, I could see why.

Shavonnia is one of the most charismatic people I have ever met. As she strode into I-ron-ic, it was obvious she had a spark that commands a room. It's an electric quality, hard to describe and impossible to teach. During her speech later that day, I watched as she zeroed in on members of the audience whose attention wavered. She made the extra effort to speak to them each one-on-one afterward. As with Ocasio-Cortez's race, the calculus wasn't about convincing potential constituents who to vote for so much as convincing them to even bother voting at all.

York came alive in the effort to elect Shavonnia, a change that manifested itself in Maddie's transformation. Together, they told me about knocking on the door of a man who said he wanted to help the campaign but didn't see the point. The Tenth District would be redrawn before the primaries, when the Pennsylvania supreme court ruled the state's map unconstitutional, but at that time it seemed to be colored the most vibrant shade of red. It seemed there was no way a progressive candidate was ever going to win the district. "I'd love to vote for you, Shavonnia," that man told her, "but I'm afraid I'm the only Democrat on this block." She informed him that, actually, he was one of nineteen. Imagine what might be possible, if only he tried talking to his neighbors about politics.

Shavonnia's campaign was about not just connecting like-minded people but reaching out to disillusioned ones. That was especially true for the black community. "People of color hadn't really been engaged directly before Shavonnia's run," one of her strategists, Ezra Kane-Salafia, told me on the phone after the campaign ended. "The idea was always, 'Why don't people show up to what we have already built?'" Shavonnia rejected that. Many marginalized York residents felt alienated. Shavonnia spoke frankly about running for Congress as a young woman of color but refused to be deterred by the added challenges.

Shavonnia's resolve resonated with people at all levels of privilege, even after she lost. Ezra took a salary cut to join her underfunded campaign, and was admittedly crushed by their defeat, which he attributes, at least partially, to bad weather. At four fifteen on the day of the primary, a tornado touched down in Pennsylvania. Shavonnia ended up losing by less than six hundred votes.

Even if they didn't win at the polls, Shovannia's campaign changed the way the people of the Tenth District think about politics. Here, finally, was a candidate who seemed to be legitimately interested in responding to the concerns of her constituents. A lot of York residents didn't even know they could ask for that before, and so they'd ignored the whole thing entirely.

Shortly after Shavonnia lost, a local high school student invited her to speak at his graduation party. She was honored but asked why. After all, she didn't win. He told her the outcome of the election didn't matter. "My friends never cared about politics before you ran," he said. "I never knew I could care about politics before you ran."

There are converts like that kid all over the Tenth District of Pennsylvania now. Maddie is considering elected office, when before a political job of any sort seemed about as reasonable as becoming an astronaut. Months after the campaign ended, people still approach Shavonnia on the street two or three times a day. A few have said, like Maddie, that they are going to consider a campaign of their own someday. All of them tell her that they are more invested in local politics than ever before. In the end, Shavonnia was able to leave her community significantly more politically aware than when she decided to run, and her losing campaign highlights the most important part of Alexandria's winning one: talking about politics invigorates the health of democracy.

I know, I know. Easier said than done, right? It is a realization fit for the I-ron-ic café that I was traveling the country attempting to figure out how to improve the way we have political conversations while failing to have one at home. I was in Anaheim, California, at the same VidCon where I met Jack, and still ignoring my parents, when I came to understand the pain at the heart of our inability to talk to one another about politics.

During a panel discussion about political coverage in the digital age, journalist academic Jeff Jarvis discussed the overall lack of principled conservative writers. It was a thoughtful statement that explored the way fringe extremists are incentivized by the mainstream media's antagonistic mode of coverage (think: CNN's red-and-blue *Brady Bunch* squares). Later, as we made our final remarks, I wrapped up with what was intended to be a cheeky callback. "And that's why there are no principled conservatives," I said, popping a fist under my chin. It was a joke, and there were light chuckles in the audience, but one man decidedly did not get it. He jumped out of his seat. It was a flashback to what I now call "the Uno Incident."

"How are you going to say there are no principled conservatives?" he yelled.

He approached the stage. The panel was over, and now the audience was standing up to go. A small crowd had assembled into a deformed semicircle around us. I should have told him to ask Jeff, that it was his point initially, that I was trying to be cute, that I was kidding. But I froze.

"How are you going to sit up there and say that?" he said, even louder this time.

I saw that I had a chance at a better response this time around. "Okay," I said, hands up in surrender. "I need your help on this. Who do you read?"

I gave him a moment to think about it. He stuttered, scrambling for an answer that wasn't going to come. The point is not that there are literally zero principled conservative writers, but that this man had been so swept up in what he thought he was supposed to think and feel that he was operating from a place of fear rather than fact. He didn't even know what he was yelling about.

It all comes back to the thing that started me on this journey: political conversation requires a shared foundation of fact. That's why Trump's gaslighting is so dangerous. His campaign of disinformation erodes the shared reality that is required as the starting point of debate.

But we have the power to restore it.

THE POWER OF TRUTH

After a talk at the University of Delaware in the fall of 2017, a sophomore asked me how to have more confidence in expressing her views. I thought about it for a moment, moved by the earnestness of her question, then realized the answer is simple: know your shit, and go from there. The only thing that ought to be required for expressing a political opinion is that you be informed. As we break the bizarre secret rules codifying the status quo, that is the only qualifying factor that you must observe.

To be quite clear, I've spent several years studying the American political language, and I'm still learning all the time. I hope for that for all of us. Being uninformed is not a reason to be scared or ashamed; it's a reason to get informed. Establishing a foundation of fact will give you the confidence you need to enter the political conversation in spite of the obstacles of the white supremacist patriarchy.

We're not always going to agree with everyone, nor are we supposed to. Interrogating the question of how we ought to live together requires us to work through disagreement in search of solutions for our political problems. Productive conflict is the centerpiece of democracy; the foundational activity of practical citizenship is building to consensus through debate. That happens at the national scale around our most divisive issues, and it must begin at a granular level, with the people we love the most. We can't do any of that without a shared foundation of fact.

That's what was so distressing to me about the Uno Incident. When they dismissed the veracity of the Associated Press report on Comey's testimony, it became clear that my mom and dad didn't understand the fundamental goal of journalism. Part of the role of the journalist is to communicate our purpose to the public we aim to serve, and it occurred to me that I had failed to do so with my own parents. When I figured that out, I was finally ready to call them.

"Lauren." My mom gasped. "It's so good to hear from you."

I winced. "Yeah, I've missed you guys, too."

"Hey, cookie," my dad said. I was on speaker.

"Dad's here, too," Mom said, lest I think a strange man was with her in the kitchen, calling me by my childhood nickname.

I admitted it had been hard for me to go so long without talking to them. They agreed. I told them the situation was complicated, and that I still had a lot to work on in therapy, but that I couldn't comply with their request: I needed to talk about politics.

"You're asking me to pretend part of me doesn't exist," I said. "I think it might help if I tell you why I do what I do as a journalist. I just need you to listen with an open mind."

My dad let out a studied "Hmm."

"The purpose of journalism is to empower people with information," I told them, taking a breath. "That is always my goal. I share my political opinion in my work, but I always make it clear whether what I am writing is analysis or a matter of fact verified through objective method. I am always working to be as transparent as possible, to make sure readers have everything they need to think for themselves. I'm not cherry-picking information to convince you to support my argument. I am representing the world and then writing analysis by making logical ethical arguments grounded in fact. It is never my goal to manipulate, and when you say 'liberal bias,' that's what that means."

They were silent, but, it seemed, thoughtfully so.

"I'm always doing my best to tell you the truth, both as a journalist and as your daughter," I said. "I hope you know that."

I held my breath.

My dad let out a sob. I always forget how easily he cries. He has a big heart, if you can get past the bouts of fire and brimstone.

"We love you so much," my mom said. "Please just know we love you."

Things have only gotten better since that call. I remember in late July 2018, my dad asked me what I thought of the Supreme Court nomination. Before, we weren't able to talk about politics without yelling. Now he was soliciting my opinion.

That summer, Justice Anthony Kennedy announced his retirement, opening the opportunity for Trump to appoint a nominee. Trump repeatedly said he would select a justice who would overturn *Roe v. Wade*. Brett Kavanaugh's judicial history was in keeping with that promise. He was chosen from a list drafted by the Federalist Society, which was launched largely in response to the *Roe* decision in 1973, in order to establish a conservative majority that would roll back reproductive rights.

"Do you really think that's something to be concerned about?" he asked me. "Don't you think *Roe* is law of the land at this point?"

He'd been reading a lot about how Kavanaugh seemed like a

good choice. (I wondered if he had read the wildly irresponsible excuse for a *Washington Post* op-ed titled "I Don't Know Kavanaugh the Judge. But Kavanaugh the Carpool Dad Is One Great Guy.")

I told my dad about Kavanaugh's record on reproductive rights and the inequity created by a lack of abortion access. (Depending on the accessibility of care in each state, terminating a pregnancy can require a woman to take off from work and drive dozens or even hundreds of miles to the nearest clinic, sometimes after shelling out to rent a car and hotel room. For women without adequate financial resources, abortion, even when it is technically legal, is only truly a matter of choice for those who can afford it.) My dad said he understood my point, but that it was the conservatives' turn to pick a judge.

"Not to get too into teams," he joked, trying his best to acknowledge our differences.

"Try not to think of it like that," I said.

Instead, I encouraged him to consider the will of the people. The Supreme Court is the single most powerful institution in the United States. The weight of any one justice is the equivalent of the voice of tens of millions of Americans in the shaping of our daily lives. No justice is nominated to the court without a majority vote from the Senate, and our senators represent us.

I hadn't even gotten into the allegations of sexual abuse from Christine Blasey Ford. Those wouldn't come up until September. Anyway, we all know how this one goes. Kavanaugh was ultimately appointed to the Supreme Court. It remains a blight on the American project that there was not a public mandate in his selection process. Whatever your thoughts on Kavanaugh, his confirmation was a failure of democracy in terms of the Senate's failure to respect public will: we are not subjects of the law, we make the law, and our elected officials would do well to remember that.

It was during that call that I realized how critical this nomination would be. A few days after my dad and I spoke, I decided to join Rise Up for Roe, organized by the nonprofit organization Demand Justice. The next month, I shared some version of the rant I initially delivered to my dad in ten cities over the course of a two-week tour.

At the time, we were in the midst of what seemed to be a Hieronymus Bosch painting of crises and scandals. The administration continued its attacks on the marginalized, perpetrating human rights abuses against immigrants, including but not limited to keeping children in cages at the US-Mexico border; undermining reproductive freedom in terms of both real and legal access to abortions across the country; and instituting an effort to dehumanize trans people by issuing an order to ban them from the military and, later, to erase them from the census. All of this occurred in conjunction with the ongoing Russia investigation, which showcased the administration's embrace of authoritarianism. Trump fired Comey in May 2017, after he refused to pledge the president his loyalty. It was later revealed that, after Comey's dismissal, two of Trump's cabinet members had said they were "willing to" invoke the Twenty-Fifth Amendment, through which the president could be deemed unfit to serve by a majority of cabinet members. The rulings of the Supreme Court would affect all of that—as well as the question of whether to block executive action on immigration, the constitutionality of *Roe v. Wade* (with which Kavanaugh had explicitly disagreed), and the constraints of executive power—for decades to come. The arc of American history would be decided, in large part, by whoever was selected to fill Kennedy's seat.

When I explained all that to my dad, he waited for me to finish before he responded. "I hadn't thought of it like that before," he said.

"You know what?" I told him. "Me either."

I didn't need him to agree with me then and there. All that mattered was that he was willing to talk and willing to listen. I was, too.

A few weeks before I was putting the final edits on this book, he sent me a post from the *Washington Examiner* to ask what I thought about Howard Schultz considering a run for office as an independent centrist.

I called to say we could totally talk about how a billionaire should not be able to hijack the presidential election, but that the article he'd sent didn't come from an objective news source. The *Washington Examiner* often approaches stories with significant right-wing bias.

"You can read it, but just know where they tend to be coming from," I said.

"I'm sorry," he said. "I'll take them off my list."

I told him not to be sorry, that the best we can do is learn, and that I was glad we were able to do that together now. And then we made plans to get brunch.

CHAPTER 8

DEMOCRACY FOR REAL

As I wrote these final pages, a friend who teaches seventh grade at a Bronx middle school asked if I would come speak to her class. She said they had a lot of tough questions for me, so I'd better be prepared. "You should see what they wrote down." She laughed. "One of them would like to know, 'How do you start a revolution?'"

If that sounds grandiose, you're not dreaming big enough. How do you start a revolution? Person by person, step by step. The paradigm shift begins in our communities. One statistically non-significant degree at a time, individual action builds to collective power. A revolution is the overthrow of the established hierarchy, and isn't that exactly what's already happening?

It's how the Parkland students have changed the conversation around gun reform and how AOC disseminates policy proposals alongside beauty advice on Instagram. It's how Heather Ward brings the student perspective to school board meetings and how James Wellemeyer created the civics textbook his peers were missing. All have rejected "the way things are." These inspiring young people are not outliers but exceptional examples of an overarching trend. Our generation wants change, and we are no longer willing to wait our turn.

This country is currently an oligarchy dressed up in a democracy costume from Party City, and that will continue to be the case, until we make a paradigmatic shift in our approach to citizenship. It is imperative that we reject the lull of the democratic bystander effect and insist on routinely and rigorously questioning who makes the rules that shape our lives. The most effective way to overthrow the political-industrial complex is by rethinking democractic citizenship as an active, ongoing process and then doing the work to uphold it.

To varying degrees, we are all complicit in the status quo. Perhaps the best way to illustrate this is through street art I once saw depicting "the machine": A Jurassic crocodile, with grinding gears where organs would be, loomed over a mob of protestors. The monster's body wrapped around the wall, dwarfing the public assembly. It was David facing off against Goliath, except David left his slingshot at home. The crocodile grinned, and as on-the-nose as this interpretation seemed to be, I felt it like a punch in the gut: the system can appear as a devastating adversary.

It was in another piece of graffiti that I found a more actionable interpretation. Instead of a reptile, this time "the man" was literalized: hundreds of bodies, writhing in pain, came together to form the shape of a giant human head. A single body dangled from a giant hand, above a giant mouth opened wide, prepared to consume a piece of itself. Again, a bit on-the-nose, but still an effective illustration: we are all part of "the way things are," and we all must contribute to the process of transformation.

The dominance of the ruling class is inevitable only so long as we fail to insist on our role within our governance. In a state of alienation, the status quo seems like the enemy. After an awakening, it's plain that we all must be part of the change we wish to see. The political-industrial complex will flourish and prosper until we come together to call bullshit.

It is crucial that we continue to question authority by insisting on our own. The power of our current moment comes from the fact that we are now redefining the meaning of citizenship as a matter of constant, active participation. As we insist on our individual agency, channeling our newfound self-determination into sustained action, we can come together to build a future in which each and every citizen has an equal voice in the political conversation.

It is a moral argument when I tell you that for true democracy, it is crucial that we are all equal stakeholders in the system of power. I could do a whole rant on the logical reasoning behind our nation's founding philosophy, but an ethical proof should not be required in order to assert the necessity of working to establish equity. Our founding fathers determined that "all men are created equal," but we're moving on from the white supremacist patriarchy together now, and the next step is to acknowledge that they ought to have said "all people." Equality is not radical; it's essential to any legitimate democratic state. I hope that, just in terms of not being a bunch of assholes, we can all agree on that.

Why would it be the case that the few have more say than the many? The duopoly conspires to frame American politics into the binary of teams. This goes on to fuel the unhealthy competition between the Democratic and Republican Parties, further fueling the political-industrial complex and diminishing public power.

I don't want to get into what a raging dumpster fire this country is at the moment, because I'd rather focus on rising out of the ashes like a goddamn phoenix. Still, ever so briefly, let's take a look at the state of our democratic culture: The tribalism of partisanship increasingly divides us. We are languishing in the bubbles of our echo chambers, online and off. Trapped by the fractured political conversation, we cling to validation in the things we think we know for sure. Accepting the lazy comfort of confirmation bias, we fall further into the tyranny of in-group/out-group dynamics, resolving to block those who disagree, as if they may as well not even exist.

It's not working. We're scared and alone, sinking ever deeper into our respective states of alienation as we are increasingly cut off from one another. The result? We've painted ourselves into a million statistically non-significant corners. We will find freedom and happiness when we strive for unity. We have to choose to participate in democracy out of duty to the collective. Truly, that's all there is.

So, there's the why of citizenship: we owe it to one another to join in on the effort of building a truer, more equitable democracy. Now, what about the how?

SO, YOU'RE AWAKE!

I figured a bunch of twelve-year-olds in the Bronx didn't want to hear me attempting to write a poem about the status quo

with the help of street art. If they were interested in starting a revolution, they needed concrete instructions to empower themselves after I left the classroom. It occurred to
me that the best way to nudge them toward political agency
would be through examples of how others have questioned
who makes the rules and then insisted on a role in deciding
"the way things are."

What should citizenship look like exactly? It should mean
actively participating in the question of how we ought to live
together. At the most basic, transactional level, citizenship requires voting, but citizenship is also an ethical model, a guiding
principle, an aesthetic, a mood, a way of existing in the world.
All of us need to be actively engaged in the political conversation, and, of course, we need to vote (rinse, repeat), but what
our individual habits look like beyond those practices will be
quite different.

There are infinite options for daily democratic action. Three
fundamental steps can help shape those habits.

I imagine this part of our story as me going into infomercial
mode: So, you're awake! Now what? Well, friends, being a good
citizen is as easy as three simple steps.

STEP #1: Learn
STEP #2: Decide
STEP #3: Act

Let's break it down.

STEP #1: LEARN—EMPOWER YOURSELF WITH INFORMATION

Practical citizenship requires a foundation of fact. Even if you didn't benefit from a rigorous civic education in school, remember that you have the tools to arm yourself with information. There are no stupid questions, just stupid people who refuse to use Google. Seriously, in the scope of human history, it has never been so easy to just look it up. That can mean a detail about a national news story or your local representatives' contact information. Decide to identify as a high-information voter.

I admit the overload of information in this political climate can be paralyzing. Following the news is part of my job, and I still struggle to keep up sometimes. You don't have to become fully versed in the political landscape overnight. Do the best you can, and accept that your knowledge will build over time. Resist the temptation to shut down on the too-much-ness we all feel, and embrace the relief of understanding yourself as a perpetual student. Heck, I'm still learning every day.

Now, you're going to need to be critical, both while determining your media diet and while engaging with it. When I get specific about the question of how to follow the news, I usually advise people to pick a core collection of established hard-news outlets and wires. I would suggest a sampling from prestige publications like the *New York Times*, the *Washington Post*, the *Wall Street Journal*, the Associated Press, Reuters, NPR, and/ or the BBC. In addition to these, I suggest reading your local newspaper in order to identify issues affecting your community, which is likely where you will have the greatest impact.

You'll note that I have taken digs at both the *Post* and the *Times* in these pages. They make mistakes sometimes, and so do I. Journalists are human beings. That's one of many reasons that you should engage with multiple sources. Compare and contrast the way various outlets cover stories. How is the story being told? What word choices are used in the headline? Have the authors been transparent about what decisions were made in the editorial process? Does any information seem to be missing?

You will likely want some commentary and analysis for deeper understanding. I tend to follow the conversation on Twitter and find myself reading from up to a dozen websites a day, but some of my favorite publications include the *New Yorker*, *New York* magazine, the *Atlantic*, the *Nation*, and, for reasons that have been specified at length, *Teen Vogue*.

When you are reading opinion writing, you need to be a critical thinker. Sometimes, commentary and analysis are more polemic than journalism, and there are times when outlets fail to clarify the distinction. In a work of polemic, the writer is attempting to convince you of a preformed idea by cherry-picking information that supports their conclusion rather than proving a thesis with clearly delineated facts and analysis. The best way to spot the difference is to ask questions, some of which I've listed above. If someone is able to change the way you think about something, ask yourself why. If you leave a piece with a new political opinion, make sure you are not blindly accepting what is fed to you. Always be certain you can show your work. If you remain unsure why you believe what you believe, you need more information.

Insist on being a critical thinker. Be rigorous in vetting what you read and in what you share. Always have receipts. Verify facts before you communicate them to friends and family, in real life or online. Journalists work to empower the public with information, but we each also hold that responsibility as citizens. Actually, I would encourage all of us to conduct ourselves in accordance with the ethics of journalism.

In keeping with his gaslighting, Trump has framed the press as "the enemy of the people," when the reality is that the fourth estate exists, first and foremost, to serve the public by providing the foundation of information required for the practice of citizenship. The post-truth state enabled by the scourge of fake news and constant disinformation disseminated by the White House makes us doubt what is and isn't true. The goal is to make us question our own sanity, to look at all the conflicting narratives and give up entirely. Journalism uses objectivity of method to verify information so that we can discuss how we ought to live together from a place of truth.

To conclude this portion of my pep talk, I leave you with a bit of Journalism 101: journalism is a tool, a human invention for building consensus around fact. Human beings have been struggling with the concept of truth since we first messed around with free time, because even the idea of truth is subjective, right? If I was writing this as a college philosophy paper, I'd probably add a quote from an ancient Greek. "Plato once said, 'Truth is the beginning of every good to the gods, and of every good to man,'" I might write in Times New Roman, font size 12. "But how can we really know the nature of truth?"

I've bullshitted my way through an epistemology seminar before. I'll save you the summary of "The Allegory of the Cave," because, really, you get it if you've played a game of telephone. The ways we perceive the world are starkly different. The best we can do is develop objectivity of method to verify information and use it to communicate with one another with respect for the highest possible standard of truth. (I kind of can't believe I'm going to bat for Enlightenment thinking in the twenty-first century, but here we are.)

Once you've built a foundation of fact, it's time for step #2.

STEP #2: DECIDE—FORM A POLITICAL OPINION

Political agency means insisting on your right to think for yourself. Once you are fully informed, be confident that you have everything you need to establish a political opinion. But it's not a done deal. Just like democracy, forming political opinions is a dynamic process that must be subject to ongoing evolution. Be willing to learn and adapt as you are introduced to new information. Be willing to question your guiding system of belief. Always be wary of that which just sort of seems true. If you start to feel like you're on shaky ground, check in on that foundation of fact. Read more. Debate more. Ask all of the questions.

I can't tell you what to believe; however, I think it is a matter of common decency to assert that when we think about the best possible future, the only way to achieve democracy is through policies of equity that build to true equality. We will most certainly have disagreements regarding the best path to that goal, but it ought to be our North Star. A lack of equality also tends to be a way of knowing that you've bumped into some of the political-industrial complex's Wizard of Oz bullshit. When only certain kinds of people are given access to the conversation, the bizarre secret rules are usually explained in a truism loop sent down from gatekeepers: that's the way things are, because they said so.

There are times when I still fall prey to the stealthy secondary effect of the vortex that dictates what is "normal" or "respectable." My right to participate in the political conversation is routinely called into question. There are myriad ways I am mocked and attacked that would never happen to my male counterparts. I find it all to be terrifically boring. Few people would be so brazen as to tell me I can't be a prominent political journalist because I'm a young woman, but you really have to ask yourself why there are so few of us. When I doubt my worthiness, I tend to correct the imposter syndrome by treating myself to some political journalism written by a mediocre man. (I especially enjoy reading Chris Cillizza—self-esteem has been an issue for me in the past, but I know I'm at least as qualified as a bowl of oatmeal.)

When you are forming your political opinions, do not be at all constrained by "the way things are." Be fearless in probing who makes the rules at every level of the hierarchy.

I find it effective to think of this in terms of Citizens United, which effectively determined that corporations are people, insofar as money is speech in our political process. That 2010 case by the Supreme Court sided with Citizens United over the Federal Election Commission, ultimately ruling that, as the SCOTUSblog states, "political spending is a form of protected speech under the First Amendment, and the government may not keep corporations or unions from spending money to support or denounce individual candidates in elections." That decision decimated the voice of the people, and yet we are meant to view it as the proper functioning of our three branches of government, because, I don't know, the manufacturer of the self-cleaning litter box says that's how it works.

The Supreme Court is the most imposing of the pillars holding up the bizarre secret rules of our oligarchy, but the judicial branch is a public institution that ought to be accountable to the people. No justice is confirmed to the court without a vote by a majority of senators, and senators are meant to vote on behalf of the people who elected them. Questioning the Supreme Court starts with holding senators accountable when they vote against the will of their constituents. You'll recall Kavanaugh's confirmation.

This conversation is ongoing and will only develop further as the partiality of the court is increasingly revealed through its reigning conservative majority. But in the immediate future, we can elect lawmakers who are invested in court reform, primarily through term limits. (Anyway, that's just a quick sampling of my personal vision board, which also features a photo of Ariana Grande shaking hands with Elizabeth Warren.)

In short, in this reckoning moment, the white supremacist capitalist patriarchy is an unraveling spool of thread that goes all the way back to the Constitution. Yeah, I said it. This country was founded by a bunch of white dudes, who, by the way, Tucker Carlson, appear to have spent an exorbitant amount of time on their hair and makeup. Questioning authority includes probing all aspects of American life, including the very basis upon which this country was founded.

Emphasizing constitutionality is the most concrete way in which we are browbeaten into ratifying a lack of solutions as "just the way things are." As with all matters of the status quo, it seems legit, until you start poking at it. What does "constitutional" mean, exactly? It should not be, as some "originalists" would have it, an insistence that things cannot change. The Constitution expressly supported the practice of slavery. Women were not given the right to vote. Native Americans were excluded entirely.

As Ruth Bader Ginsburg once said, "The genius of the United States has been its growth capacity. Recall that 'We, the People,' were once white, property-owning men. That concept, 'We, the People,' has become ever more embracive. . . . Today, 'We, the People,' has a marvelous diversity, wholly absent in the beginning."

The push for a truer, more equitable society must continue, and that includes alterations to our founding document. Even the Constitution allows for our input. Modern constitutionality is dictated by the subjective opinion of the people our senators vote to confirm to the Supreme Court. It is a feat of irrationality that we are somehow able to agree that certain portions of this nation's founding document were disgraceful while treating the rest as if it can't be subject to change. Everything can be subject to change, including the stuff a bunch of white dudes in wigs wrote on a piece of paper more than two hundred years ago.

I'm not saying that we should all chip in and get Nic Cage to steal the Constitution. But I do want us to operate out of duty to one another, honoring truth and the common good. Everything else can and will shift and change over time, including some things that are now considered "constitutional." Much of the opposition to the Parkland students' work on gun reform is grounded in an obsession with the Second Amendment, as if the right to bear arms is the end-all-be-all law of the land, except the structural absurdity of that position is right there in the name. (As the Australian comedian Jim Jefferies once observed, "It's called an 'amendment.' If you can't change something that's called an 'amendment,' see, many of you need a thesaurus more than you need a constitution.")

Once you've developed your political opinions based on a foundation of fact, it's time to raise your voice. This brings us to step 3.

STEP #3: ACT—PUT YOUR BELIEFS INTO ACTION

Expressing political opinions can come in many forms. The essential thing to understand is that you have the right to a voice. That can mean engaging in dialogue in real life or online. Raising your voice can take the form of voting, boycotting, running for office, contacting elected officials, protesting, demonstrating, marching, volunteering, donating, fundraising, organizing— the list goes on. This is the work of practical citizenship. All of those activities can be part of your habit of democracy. Political engagement must extend far beyond the acts of voting and/or showing up to jury duty, unless you define being a "good citizen" as rote obedience to the state, which isn't democracy so much as its opposite.

Instead, being a citizen of a democracy is about insisting on a right to the political conversation and, wherever possible, leveraging your privilege in pursuit of equality. Now that we see that the inevitability of the status quo is an illusion, how can we reinvigorate a sense of responsibility in demanding our rights? At the core of democratic citizenship is the duty of holding power accountable by defending the public good. There are infinite options for action to that end.

I witnessed an excellent example of this in February of 2018, when I hosted a feminist roundtable for my column at *Teen Vogue*. Everyone approached the discussion from a different background, but we were united in our desire for equity. At one end of the table was Sarah McBride, the first openly transgender person to ever address a major political convention. She sat across from Emma Sulkowicz, a performance artist who had recently protested the inclusion of alleged sexual abusers at the Met and MoMA, covering her mostly nude body in asterisks to symbolize the institution's lack of acknowledgment of survivors. Here was a woman who was working within the private industry of the two-party system, seated across from a radical activist demonstrating to raise awareness. They expressed mutual respect over their shared mission. "I have come to recognize that my skills and tactics are best built for the in-the-room kind of change," Sarah said. "But I also want people outside of the room protesting."

There is more than one way to do the damn thing. Not everyone is going to protest, and not everyone is going to run for office, but you have to do something. The young people in these pages went through a similar transformation in a different way. After their political awakening, they identified the things they cared about the most and used the things they were best at to put their beliefs into action. What are the things you care about the most? What are the things you are best at? I'd encourage you to zero in on local issues. What are ways that you might improve your community? Have you ever attended a town hall? How is civics taught in your local high school? Can you make sure everyone in your community is registered to vote?

Overall, the guiding inquiry is this: how can you turn the fight for a truer, more equitable democracy into part of your routine? We all need to develop our own acts of practical citizenship. They will look different for everyone. But we must commit to the habit of democracy.

THE HABIT OF DEMOCRACY

Here's what it looks like for me. When the switch flipped, I no longer knew how to write about anything but politics. In doing so, I was exposed to the oppressive hierarchy that defines the political conversation. I saw, with fresh eyes, how aggressively young people are dismissed and how that is compounded by sexism for young women, and by racism for people of color.

Tucker Carlson telling me to "stick to the thigh-high boots" ended up being the perfect demonstration of the bizarre secret rules that keep us from speaking up.

There tends to be a way things are done when it comes to political conversation. It's all rather joyless. If I played by the script, I would only tweet austere news updates and maybe wear unflattering suit sets from Ann Taylor LOFT. I wouldn't share anecdotes from my personal life or make jokes or curse, because those forms of expression are not typically associated with politics. I think that's a crock of shit. The political conversation can be messy and complex, and inextricably linked to the stuff we care about, be it golf or Harry Potter. The things that bring us joy can bring us power, and, even when they are genuinely frivolous, it's unreasonable for nonserious interests to disqualify people from the political conversation. We have to be able to enjoy our lives while interrogating the question of how we ought to live together.

Ever since the 2016 election, I have made an effort to share the messiness of my real life alongside serious political opinions. And, okay, fine, sometimes it's not that serious, and the reasoning behind my tweets is that I am currently high. Still, my guiding philosophy is grounded in my belief that sharing as much of my worldview with readers as possible is the closest I can get to truth. To be clear, I don't expect Associated Press reporters to start oversharing their dating history on Twitter. We have a need for hard reporting, but also journalists willing to tell their personal stories in full color. Everyone comes to such activities as writing and basic small talk with a set of preferences or the particular traumas of any given childhood. All I can do is give you information about my perspective and then do my best to tell the truth from that starting point. You should be a critical reader of my work, questioning my conclusions the same way I would recommend you question any other political journalist, and I think it's best if you know exactly where I'm coming from.

You may be wondering how any of this is allowed or whether it isn't all a bit "unprofessional." There are those bizarre secret rules again. An important thing to know about journalism is that there are no official guidelines dictating the practice. Journalists don't have to get licenses like doctors or pass an exam like lawyers. Journalism is not a profession—it's a trade. All we have are editorial standards that vary from newsroom to newsroom. As an independent freelancer, I've had to develop and maintain them for myself. I adhere to the fact-checking standards of whatever publication I am writing for, but, beyond that, I work under a set of ethical principles that define not only individual published bylines but everything I share publicly. I have a specific set of standards and practices regarding my conduct in all aspects of life and how I disclose those actions to my readers.

The old school of journalism tends to hold that you must eliminate all hint of personality, as if your worldview might be stuffed into a garbage disposal. I witnessed a particularly frustrating example of this on a Friday morning in April of 2017 at Rutgers University, where I had been invited to speak on a panel titled "Amplifying Voices: The Women Who Cover Politics." The panel was about how the female perspective shapes coverage and the ways in which politics is covered when that perspective is lacking, as is the case among the leadership in too many newsrooms. It was part of a series of discussions arranged for the Gloria Steinem Chair for Media, Culture, and Feminist Studies. Gloria was in the audience, and that made it all the more shocking when one of the other journalists declined to identify as a feminist.

"I'm a journalist," she answered when asked if she would call herself a feminist. Earlier in the panel, this journalist had discussed how she had advocated for herself amid gendered disadvantages, once receiving a promotion while on maternity leave. That sounded pretty damn feminist to me, but her answer was about the appearance of the label rather than a personal guiding philosophy. When pushed, she insisted "journalist" was the only thing she could identify as. It seemed absurd to me that declaring yourself a feminist might be anathema to journalistic standards. The purpose of journalism is empowering people with the information needed to participate in democracy. That approach doesn't only allow for advocating equality—I would argue that it requires it. Also, if you can't say that you are a feminist journalist, what else is off-limits? Can I not be objective if I tell you I like dogs better than cats? Are journalists forbidden from having a favorite color? (Short answer: No, but when describing a rainbow, it would be helpful to disclose a preference for purple rather than pretending to be color-blind.)

After the interview, Gloria came up to shake our hands. I was pinching myself. It doesn't matter, but I'll have you know that she was wearing an ombré green scarf and that she looked absolutely radiant. I thanked her for her work, for everything she's done to carry women forward. I was overwhelmed by processing an American icon as a living, breathing human being, and so perhaps that's why it fell out of my mouth, as if by accident. "I can't believe she refused to identify as a feminist," I said. Gloria sighed. "I don't know whose rules she thinks she's playing by," she said. "She didn't make those rules." And then, spotting the Chill Pills phone case I was gripping too tightly, she asked, "Did you want to take a selfie?"

On the way home, I kept thinking about the way I had allowed the unquestioned authority of gatekeepers to affect my view of journalism, in this instance and many others. I had been operating under the misconception that journalists must behave according to set standards of respectability, and it's all part of the same illusion. But, more than that, I was struck by the realization that Gloria "Feminist Icon" Steinem was once a statistically non-significant person who decided to ask who makes the rules.

That's all any of this is about, really. Revolution is a matter of regular people deciding that things can be different. Rallying for hope and change can seem like a lot of clapping for Tinker Bell, but it really is a matter of believing. I can promise that the road ahead will be rocky and that our losses will be many. Except I write with the same certainty when I say that there is real magic in collective faith. It is in choosing to believe in the power of democracy that we can finally come together to build the equitable society that we deserve.

It is incumbent on each and every one of us to believe we can and to insist that we must. Our rights require responsibilities, and it is our duty to one another to uphold them. I thought

I cared about social justice before my political awakening. I wanted to leave the world a better place than I found it, but I didn't understand that social justice requires political action. As it turns out, being a good person and being a good citizen are the same thing. Truly, if we're not actively interrogating the question of how we ought to live together, what are we even doing? If you commit to empowering yourself with information, forming a political opinion from that foundation of fact, and then routinely translating your passion into action, we can build a government truly by and for the people. This is how young people will change American politics.

That may seem idealistic, but so did lots of things, once upon a time. There is every reason to trust that the political-industrial complex will be dismantled as we come together to insist on a voice in a country striving to build democracy for real. I mean, if Donald Trump can be president, why the hell not?

ACKNOWLEDGMENTS

Writing a book is quite possibly not a sane thing for a person to do. I lost my mind on several occasions over the course of this brain marathon, and I owe an endless debt of thanks to the people who were there for me through the finish line. I'm filled with gratitude.

For Laura, my best friend in the universe, who has shown up for me so many times that our status as soulmates could withstand fact-checking. For Kris, my ex-husband, who was endlessly patient with me when I came out, and remains one of the kindest people I have ever met. For Paul, my buddy pal of a little brother, who grew up to become my real adult friend. For Evan, my beloved curmudgeon, who let me rant about my big idea over no less than twenty-seven kale salads at Westville alone. For Gabby, who inspired me with her awakening story before I had any idea what this project would look like. For Chris, who spent the better part of a year with a part-time job reminding me what the hell I was doing. For Allen, my high school partner in crime, who found his way back into my life at exactly the right time. For Emma, who has been sharing her magic with me since the moment we met. For Ellyh, who routinely inspires me to continue becoming myself. For Zeba, who taught me a level of mutual appreciation rivaled only by Leonardo DiCaprio and Kate Winslet. For Phil and Elaine, who insisted *Teen Vogue* be a space where young women are taken seriously. For Rainesford, who started out as my research assistant and became an invaluable ally. For Diego, Milagros, Sarah, Nicole, Christian, Armin, and Jessi, who held space for me to fall apart and put myself back together again. For Annie, who always reminds me to spend as much time as possible hanging out with God. For Monika, my literary agent, who took a chance on me before I had altogether too many Twitter followers. For Emily, my editor, who gave me the freedom to run and the support to make sense of everything I found once I got my footing. For my mom, who, despite our disagreements, has been insisting I am the "Michael Jordan of writing" since before I could reliably spell twelve-letter words, and for my dad, who I now regularly call to talk about politics—I love you more than words can say.

ABOUT THE AUTHOR

LAUREN DUCA is an award-winning journalist focused on destroying the white supremacist patriarchy and building equitable public power by encouraging people to pursue ethical self-determination. Duca is best known for her massively viral piece "Donald Trump Is Gaslighting America" in *Teen Vogue* and an interview with Tucker Carlson that launched her efforts fighting for young people—and especially young womxn—to insist on their right to the political conversation. Duca's writing has appeared in the *New York Times*, the *New Yorker*, *New York* magazine, and other places without "New York" in the title, including the *Independent* and *Out* magazine. She's mostly just trying to get you to follow her on Twitter: @laurenduca.